NOAM CH

INTERVIEWED BY DA

THE REAL STORY SERIES

D0051787

SECRETS, LIES AND DEMOCRACY

Secrets,
Lies and
Democracy

Noam
Chomsky

Interviewed by
David Barsamian

Odonian Press
Tucson, Arizona

Additional copies of this and other Real Story books are available from Odonian Press, Box 32375, Tucson AZ 85751 (please see the inside back cover for information on our other titles and details on ordering). To order by credit card, or for information on quantity discounts, call us at 602 296 4056 or 800 REAL STORY, or fax us at 602 296 0936.

Distribution to the book trade is through Publishers Group West, Box 8843, Emeryville CA 94662, 510 658 3453 (toll-free: 800 788 3123).

Title: Susan McCallister

Original transcripts: David Barsamian, Sandy Adler

Reorganization, editing, inside design and page layout: Arthur Naiman

Copyediting, proofreading and list of organizations: Susan McCallister, Arthur Naiman

Index: Stephen Bach, Arthur Naiman

Cover photograph: Jerry Markatos

Cover design for series: Studio Silicon

Art direction and copy for this cover: Arthur Naiman

Printing: Michelle Selby, Jim Puzey et al., Consolidated Printers, Berkeley, California

Series editor: Arthur Naiman

Odonian Press gets its name from Ursula Le Guin's wonderful novel *The Dispossessed* (though we have no connection with Ms. Le Guin or any of her publishers). The last story in her collection *The Wind's Twelve Quarters* also features the Odonians.

Odonian Press donates at least 10% of its aftertax income to organizations working for social justice.

Contents

Editor's note

This book was compiled from interviews David Barsamian conducted with Noam Chomsky on December 6, 1993 and February 1, April 11 and May 2, 1994. I organized the material into (what I hope are) coherent topics and removed—as much as possible—the repetition that inevitably crops up in widely spaced interviews like these. Then I sent the result to Chomsky and Barsamian for final corrections and changes.

Barsamian's questions appear in this typeface. Phoned-in questions from radio listeners appear in the same typeface, *but in italics.*

We've tried to define terms and identify people that may be unfamiliar the first time they're mentioned. These explanatory notes are also in this typeface and appear [inside square brackets]. If you run across a term or name you don't recognize, check the index for the first page on which it appears.

Since many readers of Chomsky's books come away from them feeling overwhelmed and despairing, the last section of this book, called *What you can do*, contains a list of 144 organizations worth investing energy in (the list begins on p. 107).

The interviews this book is based on were broadcast as part of Barsamian's Alternative Radio series, which is heard on 100 stations in the US, Canada, Europe and Australia. Alternative Radio has tapes and transcripts of hundreds of other Chomsky interviews and talks, and ones by many other fascinating speakers as well. For a free catalog, call 303 444 8788 or write 2129 Mapleton, Boulder CO 80304.

Noam Chomsky was born in Philadelphia in 1928. Since 1955, he's taught at the Massachusetts Institute of Technology, where he became a full professor at the age of 32. A major figure in twentieth-century linguistics, he's also written many books on contemporary issues (see pp. 118–19 for a list of them).

Chomsky's political talks have been heard, typically by standing-room-only audiences, all over the country and the globe, and he's received countless honors and awards. In a saner world, his tireless efforts to promote justice would have long since won him the Nobel Peace Prize.

Arthur Naiman

(OFFICE)
NOAM A. CHOMSKY
MASSACHUSETTS INSTITUTE OF TECHNOLOGY
CAMBRIDGE, MA, 02139 ↓

77 MASSACUSETTS
AVENUE

(HOME - 1991)
15 SUZANNE ROAD
LEXINGTON, MA, 02173

The US

Defective democracy

Clinton's National Security Advisor, Anthony Lake, is encouraging the enlargement of democracy overseas. Should he extend that to the US?

I can't tell you what Anthony Lake has in mind, but the concept of democracy that's been advanced is a very special one, and the more honest people on the right describe it rather accurately. For example, Thomas Carothers, who was involved in what was called the "democracy assistance project" during the Reagan administration, has written a book and several articles about it.

He says the US seeks to create a form of top-down democracy that leaves traditional structures of power—basically corporations and their allies—in effective control. Any form of democracy that leaves the traditional structures essentially unchallenged is admissible. Any form that undermines their power is as intolerable as ever.

So there's a dictionary definition of *democracy* and then a real-world definition.

The real-world definition is more or less the one Carothers describes. The dictionary definition has lots of different dimensions, but, roughly speaking, a society is democratic to the extent that people in it have meaningful opportunities to take part in the formation of public policy. There are a lot of different ways in which that can be true, but insofar as it's true, the society is democratic.

A society can have the formal trappings of democracy and not be democratic at all. The Soviet Union, for example, had elections.

The US obviously has a formal democracy with primaries, elections, referenda, recalls, and so on. But what's the content of this democracy in terms of popular participation?

Over long periods, the involvement of the public in planning or implementation of public policy has been quite marginal. This is a business-run society. The political parties have reflected business interests for a long time.

One version of this view which I think has a lot of power behind it is what political scientist Thomas Ferguson calls "the investment theory of politics." He believes that the state is controlled by coalitions of investors who join together around some common interest. To participate in the political arena, you must have enough resources and private power to become part of such a coalition.

Since the early nineteenth century, Ferguson argues, there's been a struggle for power among such groups of investors. The long periods when nothing very major seemed to be going on are simply times when the major groups of investors have seen more or less eye to eye on what public policy should look like. Moments of conflict come along when groups of investors have differing points of view.

During the New Deal, for example, various groupings of private capital were in conflict over a number of issues. Ferguson identifies a high-tech, capital-intensive, export-oriented sector that tended to be quite pro-New Deal and in favor of the reforms. They wanted an orderly work force and an opening to foreign trade.

A more labor-intensive, domestically oriented sector, grouped essentially around the National Association of Manufacturers, was strongly anti-New Deal. They didn't want any of these reform measures. (Those groups weren't the only ones involved, of course. There was the labor movement, a lot of public ferment and so on.)

You view corporations as being incompatible with democracy, and you say that if we apply the concepts that are used in political analysis, corporations are fascist. That's a highly charged term. What do you mean?

I mean fascism pretty much in the traditional sense. So when a rather mainstream person like Robert Skidelsky, the biographer of [British economist John Maynard] Keynes, describes the early postwar systems as modeled on fascism, he simply means a system in which the state integrates labor and capital under the control of the corporate structure.

That's what a fascist system traditionally was. It can vary in the way it works, but the ideal state that it aims at is absolutist—top-down control with the public essentially following orders.

Fascism is a term from the political domain, so it doesn't apply strictly to corporations, but if you look at them, power goes strictly top-down, from the board of directors to managers to lower managers and ultimately to the people on the shop floor, typists, etc. There's no flow of power or planning from the bottom up. Ultimate power resides in the hands of investors, owners, banks, etc.

People can disrupt, make suggestions, but the same is true of a slave society. People who aren't owners and investors have nothing much to say about it. They can choose to rent their labor to the corporation, or to purchase the commodities or services that it produces, or to find a place in the chain of command, but that's it. That's the totality of their control over the corporation.

That's something of an exaggeration, because corporations are subject to some legal requirements and there is some limited degree of public control. There are taxes and so on. But corporations are more totalitarian than most institutions we call totalitarian in the political arena.

Is there anything large corporate conglomerates do that has beneficial effects?

A lot of what's done by corporations will happen to have, by accident, beneficial effects for the population. The same is true of the government or anything else. But what are they trying to achieve? Not a better life for workers and the firms in which they work, but profits and market share.

That's not a big secret—it's the kind of thing people should learn in third grade. Businesses try to maximize profit, power, market share and control over the state. Sometimes what they do helps other people, but that's just by chance.

There's a common belief that, since the Kennedy assassination, business and elite power circles control our so-called democracy. Has that changed at all with the Clinton administration?

First of all, Kennedy was very pro-business. He was essentially a business candidate. His assassination had no significant effect on policy that anybody has been able to detect. (There *was* a change in policy in the early 1970s, under Nixon, but that had to do with changes in the international economy.)

Clinton is exactly what he says he is, a pro-business candidate. The *Wall Street Journal* had a very enthusiastic, big, front-page article about him right after the NAFTA vote. They pointed out that the Republicans tend to be the party of business as a whole, but that the Democrats tend to favor big business over small business. Clinton, they said, is typical of this. They quoted executives from the Ford Motor Company, the steel industry, etc. who said that this is one of the best administrations they've ever had.

The day after the House vote on NAFTA, the *New York Times* had a very revealing front-page, pro-Clinton story by their Washington correspondent, R.W. Apple. It went sort of like this: People had been criticizing Clinton because he just didn't have any principles.

He backed down on Bosnia, on Somalia, on his economic stimulus program, on Haiti, on the health program. He seemed like a guy with no bottom line at all.

Then he proved that he really was a man of principle and that he really does have backbone—by fighting for the corporate version of NAFTA. So he does have principles—he listens to the call of big money. The same was true of Kennedy.

Radio listener: I've often wondered about people who have a lot of power because of their financial resources. Is it possible to reach them with logic?

They're acting very logically and rationally in their own interests. Take the CEO of Aetna Life Insurance, who makes $23 million a year in salary alone. He's one of the guys who is going to be running our health-care program if Clinton's plan passes.

Suppose you could convince him that he ought to lobby against having the insurance industry run the health-care program, because that will be very harmful to the general population (as indeed it will be). Suppose you could convince him that he ought to give up his salary and become a working person.

What would happen then? He'd get thrown out and someone else would be put in as CEO. These are institutional problems.

Why is it important to keep the general population in line?

Any form of concentrated power doesn't want to be subjected to popular democratic control—or, for that matter, to market discipline.

That's why powerful sectors, including corporate wealth, are naturally opposed to functioning democracy, just as they're opposed to functioning markets...for themselves, at least.

It's just natural. They don't want external constraints on their capacity to make decisions and act freely.

And has that been the case?

Always. Of course, the descriptions of the facts are a little more nuanced, because modern "democratic theory" is more articulate and sophisticated than in the past, when the general population was called "the rabble." More recently, Walter Lippmann called them "ignorant and meddlesome outsiders." He felt that "responsible men" should make the decisions and keep the "bewildered herd" in line.

Modern "democratic theory" takes the view that the role of the public—the "bewildered herd," in Lippmann's words—is to be spectators, not participants. They're supposed to show up every couple of years to ratify decisions made elsewhere, or to select among representatives of the dominant sectors in what's called an "election." That's helpful, because it has a legitimizing effect.

It's very interesting to see the way this idea is promoted in the slick PR productions of the right-wing foundations. One of the most influential in the ideological arena is the Bradley Foundation. Its director, Michael Joyce, recently published an article on this. I don't know whether he wrote it or one of his PR guys did, but I found it fascinating.

It starts off with rhetoric drawn, probably consciously, from the left. When left liberals or radical activists start reading it, they get a feeling of recognition and sympathy (I suspect it's directed at them and at young people). It begins by talking about how remote the political system is from us, how we're asked just to show up every once in a while and cast our votes and then go home.

This is meaningless, the article says—this isn't real participation in the world. What we need is a functioning and active civil society in which people come together and do important things, not just this business of pushing a button now and then.

Then the article asks, How do we overcome these inadequacies? Strikingly, you don't overcome them with more active participation in the political arena. You do it by abandoning the political arena and joining the PTA and going to church and getting a job and going to the store and buying something. That's the way to become a real citizen of a democratic society.

Now, there's nothing wrong with joining the PTA. But there are a few gaps here. What happened to the political arena? It disappeared from the discussion after the first few comments about how meaningless it is.

If you abandon the political arena, somebody is going to be there. Corporations aren't going to go home and join the PTA. They're going to run things. But that we don't talk about.

As the article continues, it talks about how we're being oppressed by the liberal bureaucrats, the social planners who are trying to convince us to do something for the poor. They're the ones who are really running the country. They're that impersonal, remote, unaccountable power that we've got to get off our backs as we fulfill our obligations as citizens at the PTA and the office.

This argument isn't quite presented step-by-step like that in the article—I've collapsed it. It's very clever propaganda, well designed, well crafted, with plenty of thought behind it. Its goal is to make people as stupid, ignorant, passive and obedient as possible, while at the same time making them feel that they're somehow moving towards higher forms of participation.

In your discussions of democracy, you often refer to a couple of comments of Thomas Jefferson's.

Jefferson died on July 4, 1826—fifty years to the day after the Declaration of Independence was signed. Near the end of his life, he spoke with a mixture of concern and hope about what had been achieved, and urged the population to struggle to maintain the victories of democracy.

He made a distinction between two groups—aristocrats and democrats. Aristocrats "fear and distrust the people, and wish to draw all powers from them into the hands of the higher classes." This view is held by respectable intellectuals in many different societies today, and is quite similar to the Leninist doctrine that the vanguard party of radical intellectuals should take power and lead the stupid masses to a bright future. Most liberals are aristocrats in Jefferson's sense. [Former Secretary of State] Henry Kissinger is an extreme example of an aristocrat.

Democrats, Jefferson wrote, "identify with the people, have confidence in them, cherish and consider them as the most honest and safe, although not the most wise, depository of the public interest." In other words, democrats believe the people should be in control, whether or not they're going to make the right decisions. Democrats do exist today, but they're becoming increasingly marginal.

Jefferson specifically warned against "banking institutions and monied incorporations" (what we would now call "corporations") and said that if they grow, the aristocrats will have won and the American Revolution will have been lost. Jefferson's worst fears were realized (although not entirely in the ways he predicted).

Later on, [the Russian anarchist Mikhail] Bakunin predicted that the contemporary intellectual classes would separate into two groups (both of which are examples of what Jefferson meant by aristocrats). One group, the "red bureaucracy," would take power into their own hands and create one of the most malevolent and vicious tyrannies in human history.

The other group would conclude that power lies in the private sector, and would serve the state and private power in what we now call state capitalist societies. They'd "beat the people with the people's stick," by which he meant that they'd profess democracy while actually keeping the people in line.

You also cite [the American philosopher and educator] John Dewey. What did he have to say about this?

Dewey was one of the last spokespersons for the Jeffersonian view of democracy. In the early part of this century, he wrote that democracy isn't an end in itself, but a means by which people discover and extend and manifest their fundamental human nature and human rights. Democracy is rooted in freedom, solidarity, a choice of work and the ability to participate in the social order. Democracy produces real people, he said. That's the major product of a democratic society—real people.

He recognized that democracy in that sense was a very withered plant. Jefferson's "banking institutions and monied incorporations" had of course become vastly more powerful by this time, and Dewey felt that "the shadow cast on society by big business" made reform very difficult, if not impossible. He believed that reform may be of some use, but as long as there's no democratic control of the workplace, reform isn't going to bring democracy and freedom.

Like Jefferson and other classical liberals, Dewey recognized that institutions of private power were absolutist institutions, unaccountable and basically totalitarian in their internal structure. Today, they're far more powerful than anything Dewey dreamed of.

This literature is all accessible. It's hard to think of more leading figures in American history than Thomas Jefferson and John Dewey. They're as American as apple pie. But when you read them today, they sound like crazed Marxist lunatics. That just shows how much our intellectual life has deteriorated.

In many ways, these ideas received their earliest—and often most powerful—formulation in people like [the German intellectual] Wilhelm von Humboldt, who inspired [the English philosopher] John Stuart Mill and was one of the founders of the classical liberal tradition in the late eighteenth century. Like [the Scottish moral philosopher] Adam Smith and others, von Humboldt felt that at the root of human nature is the need for free creative work under one's own control. That must be at the basis of any decent society.

Those ideas, which run straight through to Dewey, are deeply anticapitalist in character. Adam Smith didn't call himself an anticapitalist because, back in the eighteenth century, he was basically precapitalist, but he had a good deal of skepticism about capitalist ideology and practice—even about what he called "joint stock companies" (what we call corporations today, which existed in quite a different form in his day). He worried about the separation of managerial control from direct participation, and he also feared that these joint stock companies might turn into "immortal persons."

This indeed happened in the nineteenth century, after Smith's death [under current law, corporations have even more rights than individuals, and can live forever]. It didn't happen through parliamentary decisions—nobody voted on it in Congress. In the US, as elsewhere in the world, it happened through judicial decisions. Judges and corporate lawyers simply crafted a new society in which corporations have immense power.

Today, the top two hundred corporations in the world control over a quarter of the world's total assets, and their control is increasing. *Fortune* magazine's annual listing of the top American corporations found increasing profits, increasing concentration, and reduction of jobs—tendencies that have been going on for some years.

Von Humboldt's and Smith's ideas feed directly into the socialist-anarchist tradition, into the left-libertarian critique of capitalism. This critique can take the Deweyian form of a sort of workers'-control version of democratic socialism, or the left-Marxist form of people like [the Dutch astronomer and political theorist] Anton Pannekoek and [the Polish-German revolutionary] Rosa Luxemburg, or [the leading anarchist] Rudolf Rocker's anarcho-syndicalism (among others).

All this has been grossly perverted or forgotten in modern intellectual life but, in my view, these ideas grow straight out of classical, eighteenth-century liberalism. I even think they can be traced back to seventeenth-century rationalism.

Keeping the rich on welfare

A book called *America: Who Pays the Taxes?*, written by a couple of *Philadelphia Inquirer* reporters, apparently shows that the amount of taxes paid by corporations has dramatically declined in the US.

That's for sure. It's been very striking over the last fifteen years.

Some years ago, a leading specialist, Joseph Pechman, pointed out that despite the apparently progressive structure that's built into the income tax system (that is, the higher your income, the higher your tax rate), all sorts of other regressive factors end up making everyone's tax rate very near a fixed percentage.

An interesting thing happened in Alabama involving Daimler-Benz, the big German auto manufacturer.

Under Reagan, the US managed to drive labor costs way below the level of our competitors (except for Britain). That's produced consequences not only in Mexico and the US but all across the industrial world.

For example, one of the effects of the so-called free trade agreement with Canada was to stimulate a big flow of jobs from Canada to the southeast US, because that's an essentially nonunion area. Wages are lower; you don't have to worry about benefits; workers can barely organize. So that's an attack against Canadian workers.

Daimler-Benz, which is Germany's biggest conglomerate, was seeking essentially Third World conditions. They managed to get our southeastern states to compete against one another to see who could force the public to pay the largest bribe to bring them there. Alabama won. It offered hundreds of millions of dollars in tax benefits, practically gave Daimler-Benz the land on which to construct their plant, and agreed to build all sorts of infrastructure for them.

Some people will benefit—the small number who are employed at the plant, with some spillover to hamburger stands and so on, but primarily bankers, corporate lawyers, people involved in investment and financial services. They'll do very well, but the cost to most of the citizens of Alabama will be substantial.

Even the *Wall Street Journal,* which is rarely critical of business, pointed out that this is very much like what happens when rich corporations go to Third World countries, and it questioned whether there were going to be overall benefits for the state of Alabama. Meanwhile Daimler-Benz can use this to drive down the lifestyle of German workers.

German corporations have also set up factories in the Czech Republic, where they can get workers for about 10% the cost of German workers. The Czech Republic is right across the border; it's a Westernized society with high educational levels and nice white people with blue eyes. Since they don't believe in the free market any more than any other rich people do, they'll leave the Czech Republic to pay the social costs, pollution, debts and so on, while they pick up the profits.

It's exactly the same with the plants GM is building in Poland, where it's insisting on 30% tariff protection. The free market is for the poor. We have a dual system—protection for the rich and market discipline for everyone else.

I was struck by an article in the *New York Times* whose headline was, "Nation considers means to dispose of its plutonium." So the nation has to figure out how to dispose of what was essentially created by private capital.

That's the familiar idea that profits are privatized but costs are socialized. The costs are the nation's, the people's, but the profits weren't for the people, nor did they make the decision to produce plutonium in the first place, nor are they making the decisions about how to dispose of it, nor do they get to decide what ought to be a reasonable energy policy.

One of the things I've learned from working with you is the importance of reading *Business Week, Fortune* and the *Wall Street Journal.* In the business section of the *New York Times,* I read a fascinating discussion by a bureaucrat from MITI [Japan's Ministry of International Trade and Industry] who trained at the Harvard Business School.

One of his classes was studying a failed airline that went out of business. They were shown a taped interview with the company's president, who noted with pride that through the whole financial crisis and eventual bankruptcy of the airline, he'd never asked for government help. To the Japanese man's astonishment, the class erupted into applause.

He commented, "There's a strong resistance to government intervention in America. I understand that. But I was shocked. There are many shareholders in companies. What happened to his employees, for example?" Then he reflects on what he views as America's blind devotion to a free-market ideology. He says, "It is something quite close to a religion. You cannot argue about it with most people. You believe it or you don't." It's interesting.

It's interesting, in part, because of the Japanese man's failure to understand what actually happens in the US, which apparently was shared by the students in his business class. If it was Eastern Airlines they were talking about, Frank Lorenzo, the director, was trying to put it out of business. He made a personal profit out of that.

He wanted to break the unions in order to support his other enterprises (which he ripped off profits from Eastern Airlines for). He wanted to leave the airline industry less unionized and more under corporate control, and to leave himself wealthier. All of that happened. So naturally he didn't call on government intervention to save him—things were working the way he wanted.

On the other hand, the idea that corporations don't ask for government help is a joke. They demand an extraordinary amount of government intervention. That's largely what the whole Pentagon system is about.

Take the airline industry, which was created by government intervention. A large part of the reason for the huge growth in the Pentagon in the late 1940s was to salvage the collapsing aeronautical industry, which obviously couldn't survive in a civilian market. That's worked—it's now the United States' leading export industry, and Boeing is the leading exporter.

An interesting and important book on this by Frank Kofsky just came out. It describes the war scares that were manipulated in 1947 and 1948 to try to ram spending bills through Congress to save the aeronautical industry. (That wasn't the only purpose of these war scares, but it was a big factor.)

Huge industries were spawned, and are maintained, by massive government intervention. Many corporations couldn't survive without it. (For some, it's not a huge part of their profits at the moment, but it's a cushion.) The public also provides the basic technology—metallurgy, avionics or whatever—via the public subsidy system.

The same is true just across the board. You can hardly find a functioning sector of the US manufacturing or service economy which hasn't gotten that way and isn't sustained by government intervention.

The Clinton administration has been pouring new funds into the National Bureau of Standards and Technology. It used to try to work on how long a foot is but it will now be more actively involved in serving the needs of private capital. Hundreds of corporations are beating on their doors asking for grants.

The idea is to try to replace the somewhat declining Pentagon system. With the end of the Cold War, it's gotten harder to maintain the Pentagon system, but you've got to keep the subsidy going to big corporations. The public has to pay the research and development costs.

The idea that a Japanese investigator could fail to see this is fairly remarkable. It's pretty well known in Japan.

Health care

I don't suppose you can see the Boston skyline from your home in Lexington. But if you could, what would be the two tallest buildings?

The John Hancock and the Prudential.

And they happen to be two types of what?

They're going to be running our health-care program if Clinton has his way.

There's a general consensus that the US health-care system needs to be reformed. How did that consensus evolve?

It evolved very simply. We have a relatively privatized health-care system. As a result, it's geared towards high-tech intervention rather than public health and prevention. It's also hopelessly inefficient and extremely bureaucratic, with huge administrative expenses.

This has gotten just too costly for American business. In fact, a bit to my surprise, *Business Week*, the main business journal, has come out recently with several articles advocating a Canadian-style, single-payer program. Under this system, health care is individual, but the government is the insurer. Similar plans exist in every industrial country in the world, except the US.

The Clinton plan is called "managed competition." What is that, and why are the big insurance companies supporting it?

"Managed competition" means that big insurance companies will put together huge conglomerates of health-care institutions, hospitals, clinics, labs and so on. Various bargaining units will be set up to determine which of these conglomerates to work with. That's supposed to introduce some kind of market forces.

But a very small number of big insurance conglomerates, in limited competition with one another, will be pretty much in charge of organizing your health care. (This plan will drive the little insurance companies out of the market, which is why they're opposed to it.)

Since they're in business for profit, not for your comfort, the big insurance companies will doubtlessly micromanage health care, in an attempt to reduce it to the lowest possible level. They'll also tend away from prevention and public health measures, which aren't their concern. Enormous inefficiencies will be involved—huge profits, advertising costs, big corporate salaries and other corporate amenities, big bureaucracies that control in precise detail what doctors and nurses do and don't do—and we'll have to pay for all that.

There's another point that ought to be mentioned. In a Canadian-style, government-insurance system, the costs are distributed in the same way that taxes are. If the tax system is progressive—that is, if rich people pay a higher percentage of their income in taxes (which all other industrial societies assume, correctly, to be the only ethical approach)—then the wealthy will also pay more of the costs of health care.

But the Clinton program, and all the others like it, are radically regressive. A janitor and a CEO pay the same amount. It's as if they were both taxed the same amount, which is unheard of in any civilized society.

Actually, it's even worse than that—the janitor will probably pay more. He'll be living in a poor neighborhood and the executive will be living in a rich suburb or a downtown highrise, which means they'll belong to different health groupings. Because the grouping the janitor belongs to will include many more poor and high-risk people, the insurance companies will demand higher rates from it than the one the executive belongs to, which will include mostly wealthier, lower-risk people.

According to a Harris poll, Americans prefer the Canadian-style health-care system by a huge majority. That's kind of remarkable, given the minimal amount of media attention the single-payer system has received.

The best work I know on this is by [Professor] Vicente Navarro [of Johns Hopkins]. He's discovered that there's been quite consistent support for something like a Canadian-style system ever since polls began on this issue, which is now over forty years.

Back in the 1940s, Truman tried to put through such a program. It would have brought the US into line with the rest of the industrial world, but it was beaten back by a huge corporate offensive, complete with tantrums about how we were going to turn into a Bolshevik society and so on.

Every time the issue has come up, there's been a major corporate offensive. One of Ronald Reagan's great achievements back in the late 1960s was to give somber speeches (written for him by the AMA) about how if the legislation establishing Medicare was passed, we'd all be telling our children and grandchildren decades hence what freedom used to be like.

Steffie Woolhandler and David Himmelstein [both of Harvard Medical School] also cite another poll result: When Canadians were asked if they'd want a US-style system, only 5% said yes.

By now, even large parts of the business community don't want it. It's just too inefficient, too bureaucratic and too costly for them. The auto companies estimated a couple of years ago that it was costing them about $500 extra per car just because of the inefficiencies of the US health system—as compared with, say, their Canadian operations.

When business starts to get hurt, then the issue moves into the public agenda. The public has been in favor of a big change for a long time, but what the public thinks doesn't matter much.

There was a nice phrase about this sort of thing in the *Economist* [a leading London business journal]. The *Economist* was concerned about the fact that Poland has degenerated into a system where they have democratic elections, which is sort of a nuisance.

The population in all of the East European countries is being smashed by the economic changes that are being rammed down their throats. (These changes are called "reforms," which is supposed to make them sound good.) In the last election, the Poles voted in an anti-"reform" government. The *Economist* pointed out that this really wasn't too troublesome because "policy is insulated from politics." In their view, that's a good thing.

In this country too, policy is insulated from politics. People can have their opinions; they can even vote if they like. But policy goes on its merry way, determined by other forces.

What the public wants is called "politically unrealistic." Translated into English, that means the major centers of power and privilege are opposed to it. A change in our health-care system has now become politically more realistic because the corporate community wants a change, since the current system is harming them.

Vicente Navarro says that a universal and comprehensive health-care program is "directly related to the strength of the working class and its political and economic instruments."

That's certainly been true in Canada and Europe. Canada had a system rather like ours up until the mid-1960s. It was changed first in one province, Saskatchewan, where the NDP [the New Democratic Party, a mildly reformist, umbrella political party with labor backing] was in power.

The NDP was able to put through a provincial insurance program, driving the insurance companies out of the health-care business. It turned out to be very successful. It was giving good medical care and reducing costs and was much more progressive in payment. It was mimicked by other provinces, also under labor pressure, often using the NDP as an instrument. Pretty soon it was adopted across Canada nationally.

The history in Europe is pretty much the same. Working-class organizations have been one of the main (although not the only) mechanisms by which people with very limited power and resources can get together to participate in the public arena. That's one of the reasons unions are so hated by business and elites generally. They're just too democratizing in their character.

So Navarro is surely right. The strength and organization of labor and its ability to enter into the public arena is certainly related— maybe even decisively related—to the establishment of social programs of this kind.

There may be a parallel movement going on in California, where there's a ballot initiative to have single-payer health care.

The situation in the US is a little different from what Navarro described, because business still plays an inordinate role here in determining what kind of system will evolve. Unless there are significant changes in the US—that is, unless public pressure and organizations, including labor, do a lot more than they've done so far—the outcome will once again be determined by business interests.

Much more media attention has been paid to AIDS than to breast cancer, but a half a million women in the US will die from breast cancer in the 1990s. Many men will die from prostate cancer. These aren't considered political questions, are they?

Well, there's no vote taken on them, but if you're asking if there are questions of policy involved, of course there are. You might add to those cancers the number of children who will suffer or die because of extremely poor conditions in infancy and childhood.

Take, say, malnutrition. That decreases life span quite considerably. If you count that up in deaths, it outweighs anything you're talking about. I don't think many people in the public health field would question the conclusion that the major contribution to improving health, reducing mortality figures and improving the quality of life, would come from simple public health measures like ensuring people adequate nutrition and safe and healthy conditions of life, clean water, effective sewage treatment, and so on.

You'd think that in a rich country like this, these wouldn't be big issues, but they are for a lot of the population. *Lancet,* the British medical journal—the most prestigious medical journal in the world—recently pointed out that 40% of children in New York City live below the poverty line. They suffer from malnutrition and other poor conditions that cause very high mortality rates—and, if they survive, they have very severe health problems all through their lives.

The *New England Journal of Medicine* pointed out a couple of years ago that black males in Harlem have about the same mortality rate as people in Bangladesh. That's essentially because of the extreme deterioration of the most elementary public health conditions, and social conditions.

Some people have linked the increase in breast cancer and prostate cancer to environmental degradation, to diet, and to the increase of additives and preservatives. What do you think about that?

It's doubtless some kind of a factor. How big or serious a factor it is I'm not sure.

Are you at all interested in the so-called natural or organic food movement?

Sure. I think there ought to be concerns about the quality of food. This I would say falls into the question of general public health. It's like having good water and good sewage and making sure that people have enough food and so on.

All these things are in roughly the same category—they don't have to do with high-technology medical treatment but with essential conditions of life. These general public-health issues, of which eating food that doesn't contain poisons is naturally a part, are the overwhelming factors in quality of life and mortality.

Crime and punishment

There's been a tendency over the last few years for local TV news programs to concentrate on crimes, rapes, kidnappings, etc. Now this is spilling over into the national network news programs.

That's true, but it's just a surface phenomenon. Why is there an increase in attention to violent crime? Is it connected to the fact that there's been a considerable decline in income for the large majority of the population, and a decline as well in the opportunity for constructive work?

But until you ask why there's an increase in social disintegration, and why more and more resources are being directed towards the wealthy and privileged sectors and away from the general population, you can't have even a concept of why there's rising crime or how you should deal with it.

Over the past twenty or thirty years, there's been a considerable increase in inequality. This trend accelerated during the Reagan years. The society has been moving visibly towards a kind of Third World model.

The result is an increasing crime rate, as well as other signs of social disintegration. Most of the crime is poor people attacking each other, but it spills over to more privileged sectors. People are very worried—and quite properly, because the society is becoming very dangerous.

A constructive approach to the problem would require dealing with its fundamental causes, but that's off the agenda, because we must continue with a social policy that's aimed at strengthening the welfare state for the rich.

The only kind of responses the government can resort to under those conditions is pandering to the fear of crime with increasing harshness, attacking civil liberties and attempting to control the poor, essentially by force.

Do you know what "smash and grab" is? When your car is in traffic or at a stop light, people come along, smash in the window and grab your purse or steal your wallet.

The same thing is going on right around Boston. There's also a new form, called "Good Samaritan robbery." You fake a flat tire on the highway and when somebody stops to help, you jump them, steal their car, beat them up if they're lucky, kill them if they're not.

The causes are the increasing polarization of the society that's been going on for the past twenty-five years, and the marginalization of large sectors of the population. Since they're superfluous for wealth production (meaning profit production), and since the basic ideology is that a person's human rights depend on what they can get for themselves in the market system, they have no human value.

Larger and larger sectors of the population have no form of organization and no viable, constructive way of reacting, so they pursue the available options, which are often violent. To a large extent, those are the options that are encouraged in the popular culture.

You can tell a great deal about a society when you look at its system of justice. I was wondering if you'd comment on the Clinton crime bill, which authorizes hiring 100,000 more cops, boot camps for juveniles, more money for prisons, extending the death penalty to about fifty new offenses and making gang membership a federal crime—which is interesting, considering there's something about freedom of association in the Bill of Rights.

It was hailed with great enthusiasm by the far right as the greatest anticrime bill ever. It's certainly the most *extraordinary* crime bill in history. It's greatly increased, by a factor of five or six, federal spending for repression.

There's nothing much constructive in it. There are more prisons, more police, heavier sentences, more death sentences, new crimes, three strikes and you're out.

It's unclear how much pressure and social decline and deterioration people will accept. One tactic is just drive them into urban slums—concentration camps, in effect—and let them prey on one another. But they have a way of breaking out and affecting the interests of wealthy and privileged people. So you have to build up the jail system, which is incidentally also a shot in the arm for the economy.

It's natural that Clinton picked up this crime bill as a major social initiative, not only for a kind of ugly political reason—namely, that it's easy to whip up hysteria about it— but also because it reflects the general point of view of the so-called New Democrats, the business-oriented segment of the Democratic Party to which Clinton belongs.

What are your views on capital punishment?

It's a crime. I agree with Amnesty International on that one, and indeed with most of the world. The state should have no right to take people's lives.

Radio listener: Does this country have a vested interest in supporting the drug trade?

It's complicated; I don't want to be too brief about it. For one thing, you can't talk about marijuana and cocaine in the same breath. Marijuana simply doesn't have the lethal effects of cocaine. You can debate about whether marijuana is good or bad, but out of about sixty million users, I don't think there's a known case of overdose. The criminalization of marijuana has motives other than concern about drugs.

On the other hand, hard drugs, to which people have been driven to a certain extent by the prohibitions against soft drugs, are very harmful—although nowhere near the harm of, say, tobacco and alcohol in terms of overall societal effects, including deaths.

There are sectors of American society that profit from the hard drug trade, like the big international banks that do the money laundering or the corporations that provide the chemicals for the industrial production of hard drugs. On the other hand, people who live in the inner cities are being devastated by them. So there are different interests.

Gun control

Advocates of free access to arms cite the Second Amendment. Do you believe that it permits unrestricted, uncontrolled possession of guns?

It's pretty clear that, taken literally, the Second Amendment doesn't permit people to have guns. But laws are never taken literally, including amendments to the Constitution or constitutional rights. Laws permit what the tenor of the times interprets them as permitting.

But underlying the controversy over guns are some serious questions. There's a feeling in the country that people are under attack. I think they're misidentifying the source of the attack, but they do feel under attack.

The government is the only power structure that's even partially accountable to the population, so naturally the business sectors want to make that the enemy—not the corporate system, which is totally unaccountable. After decades of intensive business propaganda, people feel that the government is some kind of enemy and that they have to defend themselves from it.

It's not that that doesn't have its justifications. The government *is* authoritarian and commonly hostile to much of the population. But it's partially influenceable—and potentially very influenceable—by the general population.

Many people who advocate keeping guns have fear of the government in the back of their minds. But that's a crazy response to a real problem.

Do the media foster the feeling people have that they're under attack?

At the deepest level, the media contribute to the sense that the government is the enemy, and they suppress the sources of real power in the society, which lie in the totalitarian institutions—the corporations, now international in scale—that control the economy and much of our social life. In fact, the corporations set the conditions within which the government operates, and control it to a large extent.

The picture presented in the media is constant, day after day. People simply have no awareness of the system of power under which they're suffering. As a result—as intended—they turn their attention against the government.

People have all kinds of motivations for opposing gun control, but there's definitely a sector of the population that considers itself threatened by big forces, ranging from the Federal Reserve to the Council on Foreign Relations to big government to who knows what, and they're calling for guns to protect themselves.

Radio listener: On the issue of gun control, I believe that the US is becoming much more like a Third World country, and nothing is necessarily going to put a stop to it. I look around and see a lot of Third World countries where, if the citizens had weapons, they wouldn't have the government they've got. So I think that maybe people are being a little short-sighted in arguing for gun control and at the same time realizing that the government they've got is not exactly a benign one.

Your point illustrates exactly what I think is a major fallacy. The government is far from benign—that's true. On the other hand, it's at least partially accountable, and it can become as benign as we make it.

What's not benign (what's extremely harmful, in fact) is something you didn't mention—business power, which is highly concentrated and, by now, largely transnational. Business power is very far from benign and it's completely unaccountable. It's a totalitarian system that has an enormous effect on our lives. It's also the main reason why the government isn't benign.

As for guns being the way to respond to this, that's outlandish. First of all, this is not a weak Third World country. If people have pistols, the government has tanks. If people get tanks, the government has atomic weapons. There's no way to deal with these issues by violent force, even if you think that that's morally legitimate.

Guns in the hands of American citizens are not going to make the country more benign. They're going to make it more brutal, ruthless and destructive. So while one can recognize the motivation that lies behind some of the opposition to gun control, I think it's sadly misguided.

Becoming a Third World country

A recent Census Bureau report stated that there's been a 50% increase in the working poor—that is, people who have jobs but are still below the poverty level.

That's part of the Third-Worldization of the society. It's not just unemployment, but also wage reduction. Real wages have been declining since the late 1960s. Since 1987, they've even been declining for college-educated people, which was a striking shift.

There's supposed to be a recovery going on, and it's true that a kind of recovery is going on. It's at about half the rate of preceding postwar recoveries from recession (there've been half a dozen of them) and the rate of job creation is less than a third. Furthermore— out of line with earlier recoveries—the jobs themselves are low-paying, and a huge number of them are temporary.

This is what's called "increasing flexibility of the labor market." *Flexibility* is a word like reform—it's supposed to be a good thing. Actually, *flexibility* means insecurity. It means you go to bed at night and don't know if you'll have a job in the morning. Any economist can explain that that's a good thing for the economy—that is, for profit-making, not for the way people live.

Low wages also increase job insecurity. They keep inflation low, which is good for people who have money—bondholders, say. Corporate profits are zooming, but for most of the population, things are grim. And grim circumstances, without much prospect for a future or for constructive social action, express themselves in violence.

It's interesting that you should say that. Most of the examples of mass murders are in the workplace. I'm thinking of the various killings in post offices and fast-food restaurants, where workers are disgruntled for one reason or another, or have been fired or laid off.

Not only have real wages stagnated or declined, but working conditions have gotten much worse. You can see that just in counting hours of work. Julie Schor, an economist at Harvard, brought out an important book on this a couple of years ago, called *The Overworked American*. If I remember her figures correctly, by around 1990, the time she was writing, workers had to put in about six weeks extra work a year to maintain something like a 1970 real wage level.

Along with the increasing hours of work comes increasing harshness of work conditions, increasing insecurity and, because of the decline of unions, reduced ability to protect oneself. In the Reagan years, even the minimal government programs for protecting workers against workplace accidents and the like were reduced, in the interest of maximizing profits. The absence of constructive options, like union organizing, leads to violence.

Labor

[Harvard professor] Elaine Bernard and [union official] Tony Mazzocchi have been talking about creating a new labor-based party. What are your views on that?

I think that's an important initiative. The US is becoming very depoliticized and negative. About half the population thinks both political parties should be disbanded. There's a real need for something that would articulate the concerns of that substantial majority of the population that's being left out of social planning and the political process.

Labor unions have often been a significant force—in fact, the main social force—for democratization and progress. On the other hand, when they aren't linked to the political system through a labor-based party, there's a limit on what they can do. Take health care, for example.

Powerful unions in the US were able to get fairly reasonable health-care provisions for themselves. But since they were acting independently of the political system, they typically didn't attempt to bring about decent health conditions for the general population. Compare Canada, where the unions, being linked to labor-based parties, were able to implement health care for everybody.

That's an illustration of the kind of difference a politically oriented, popular movement like labor can achieve. We're not in the day any longer where the industrial workers are the majority or even the core of the labor force. But the same questions arise. I think Bernard and Mazzocchi are on the right track in thinking along those lines.

Yesterday was May 1. What's its historical significance?

It's May Day, which throughout the world has been a working-class holiday for more than a hundred years. It was initiated in solidarity with American workers who, back in the 1880s, were suffering unusually harsh conditions in their effort to achieve an eight-hour workday. The US is one of the few countries where this day of solidarity with US labor is hardly even known.

This morning, way in the back of the *Boston Globe,* there was a little item whose headline read, "May Day Celebration in Boston." I was surprised, because I don't think I've ever seen that here in the US. It turned out that there indeed was a May Day celebration, of the usual kind, but it was being held by Latin American and Chinese workers who've recently immigrated here.

That's a dramatic example of the efficiency with which business controls US ideology, of how effective its propaganda and indoctrination have been in depriving people of any awareness of their own rights and history. You have to wait for poor Latino and Chinese workers to celebrate an international holiday of solidarity with American workers.

In his *New York Times* column, Anthony Lewis wrote: "Unions in this country, sad to say, are looking more and more like the British unions...backward, unenlightened....The crude, threatening tactics used by unions to make Democratic members of the House vote against NAFTA underline the point."

That brings out Lewis's real commitments very clearly. What he called "crude, threatening tactics" were labor's attempt to get their representatives to represent their interests. By the standards of the elite, that's an attack on democracy, because the political system is supposed to be run by the rich and powerful.

Corporate lobbying vastly exceeded labor lobbying, but you can't even talk about it in the same breath. It wasn't considered raw muscle or antidemocratic. Did Lewis have a column denouncing corporate lobbying for NAFTA?

I didn't see it.

I didn't see it either.

Things reached the peak of absolute hysteria the day before the vote. The *New York Times* lead editorial was exactly along the lines of that quote from Lewis, and it included a little box that listed the dozen or so representatives in the New York region who were voting against NAFTA. It showed their contributions from labor and said that this raises ominous questions about the political influence of labor, and whether these politicians are being honest, and so on.

As a number of these representatives later pointed out, the *Times* didn't have a box listing corporate contributions to them or to other politicians—nor, we may add, was there a box listing advertisers of the *New York Times* and their attitudes towards NAFTA.

It was quite striking to watch the hysteria that built up in privileged sectors, like the *Times'* commentators and editorials, as the NAFTA vote approached. They even allowed themselves the use of the phrase "class lines." I've never seen that in the *Times* before. You're usually not allowed to admit that the US has class lines. But this was considered a really serious issue, and all bars were let down.

The end result is very intriguing. In a recent poll, about 70% of the respondents said they were opposed to the actions of the labor movement against NAFTA, but it turned out that they took pretty much the same position that labor took. So why were they opposed to it?

I think it's easy to explain that. The media scarcely reported what labor was actually *saying.* But there was plenty of hysteria about labor's alleged tactics.

The CIA

What about the role of the CIA in a democratic society? Is that an oxymoron?

You could imagine a democratic society with an organization that carries out intelligence-gathering functions. But that's a very minor part of what the CIA does. Its main purpose is to carry out secret and usually illegal activities for the executive branch, which wants to keep these activities secret because it knows that the public won't accept them. So even inside the US, it's highly undemocratic.

The activities that it carries out are quite commonly efforts to undermine democracy, as in Chile through the 1960s into the early 1970s [described on pp. 91–95]. That's far from the only example. By the way, although most people focus on Nixon's and Kissinger's involvement with the CIA, Kennedy and Johnson carried out similar policies.

Is the CIA an instrument of state policy, or does it formulate policy on its own?

You can't be certain, but my own view is that the CIA is very much under the control of executive power. I've studied those records fairly extensively in many cases, and it's very rare for the CIA to undertake initiatives on its own.

It often looks as though it does, but that's because the executive wants to preserve deniability. The executive branch doesn't want to have documents lying around that say, I told you to murder Lumumba, or to overthrow the government of Brazil, or to assassinate Castro.

So the executive branch tries to follow policies of plausible deniability, which means that messages are given to the CIA to do things but without a paper trail, without a record. When the story comes out later, it looks as if the CIA is doing things on their own. But if you really trace it through, I think this almost never happens.

The media

Let's talk about media and democracy. In your view, what are the communications requirements of a democratic society?

I agree with Adam Smith on this—we'd like to see a tendency toward equality. Not just equality of opportunity, but actual equality—the ability, at every stage of one's existence, to access information and make decisions on the basis of it. So a democratic communications system would be one that involves large-scale public participation, and that reflects both public interests and real values like truth, integrity and discovery.

Bob McChesney, in his recent book *Telecommunications, Mass Media and Democracy*, details the debate between 1928 and 1935 for control of radio in the US. How did that battle play out?

That's a very interesting topic, and he's done an important service by bringing it out. It's very pertinent today, because we're involved in a very similar battle over this so-called "information superhighway."

In the 1920s, the first major means of mass communication since the printing press came along—radio. It's obvious that radio is a bounded resource, because there's only a fixed bandwidth. There was no question in anyone's mind that the government was going to have to regulate it. The question was, What form would this government regulation take?

Government could opt for public radio, with popular participation. This approach would be as democratic as the society is. Public radio in the Soviet Union would have been totalitarian, but in, say, Canada or England, it would be partially democratic (insofar as those societies are democratic).

That debate was pursued all over the world—at least in the wealthier societies, which had the luxury of choice. Almost every country (maybe every one—I can't think of an exception) chose public radio, while the US chose private radio. It wasn't 100%; you were allowed to have small radio stations—say, a college radio station—that can reach a few blocks. But virtually all radio in the US was handed over to private power.

As McChesney points out, there was a considerable struggle about that. There were church groups and some labor unions and other public interest groups that felt that the US should go the way the rest of the world was going. But this is very much a business-run society, and they lost out.

Rather strikingly, business also won an ideological victory, claiming that handing radio over to private power constituted democracy, because it gave people choices in the marketplace. That's a very weird concept of democracy, since your power depends on the number of dollars you have, and your choices are limited to selecting among options that are highly structured by the real concentrations of power. But this was nevertheless widely accepted, even by liberals, as the democratic solution. By the mid- to late 1930s, the game was essentially over.

This struggle was replayed—in the rest of the world, at least—about a decade later, when television came along. In the US this wasn't a battle at all; TV was completely commercialized without any conflict. But again, in most other countries—or maybe every other country—TV was put in the public sector.

In the 1960s, television and radio became partly commercialized in other countries; the same concentration of private power that we find in the US was chipping away at the public-service function of radio and television. At the same time in the US, there was a slight opening to public radio and television.

The reasons for this have never been explored in any depth (as far as I know), but it appears that the private broadcasting companies recognized that it was a nuisance for them to have to satisfy the formal requirements of the Federal Communications Commission that they devote part of their programming to public-interest purposes. So CBS, say, had to have a big office with a lot of employees who every year would put together a collection of fraudulent claims about how they'd met this legislative condition. It was a pain in the neck.

At some point, they apparently decided that it would be easier to get the entire burden off their backs and permit a small and under-funded public broadcasting system. They could then claim that they didn't have to fulfill this service any longer. That was the origin of public radio and television—which is now largely corporate-funded in any event.

That's happening more and more. PBS [the Public Broadcasting Service] is sometimes called "the Petroleum Broadcasting Service."

That's just another reflection of the interests and power of a highly class-conscious business system that's always fighting an intense class war. These issues are coming up again with respect to the Internet [a worldwide computer network] and the new interactive communications technologies. And we're going to find exactly the same conflict again. It's going on right now.

I don't see why we should have had any long-term hopes for something different. Commercially run radio is going to have certain purposes—namely, the ones determined by people who own and control it.

As I mentioned earlier, they don't want decision-makers and participants; they want a passive, obedient population of consumers and political spectators—a community of people who are so atomized and isolated that they can't put together their limited resources and become an independent, powerful force that will chip away at concentrated power.

Does ownership always determine content?

In some far-reaching sense it does, because if content ever goes beyond the bounds owners will tolerate, they'll surely move in to limit it. But there's a fair amount of flexibility.

Investors don't go down to the television studio and make sure that the local talk-show host or reporter is doing what they want. There are other, subtler, more complex mechanisms that make it fairly certain that the people on the air will do what the owners and investors want. There's a whole, long, filtering process that makes sure that people only rise through the system to become managers, editors, etc., if they've internalized the values of the owners.

At that point, they can describe themselves as quite free. So you'll occasionally find some flaming independent-liberal type like Tom Wicker who writes, Look, nobody tells me what to say. I say whatever I want. It's an absolutely free system.

And, for *him*, that's true. After he'd demonstrated to the satisfaction of his bosses that he'd internalized their values, he was entirely free to write whatever he wanted.

Both PBS and NPR [National Public Radio] frequently come under attack for being left-wing.

That's an interesting sort of critique. In fact, PBS and NPR are elite institutions, reflecting by and large the points of view and interests of wealthy professionals who are very close to business circles, including corporate executives. But they happen to be liberal by certain criteria.

That is, if you took a poll among corporate executives on matters like, say, abortion rights, I presume their responses would be what's called liberal. I suspect the same would be true on lots of social issues, like civil rights and freedom of speech. They tend not to be fundamentalist, born-again Christians, for example, and they might tend to be more opposed to the death penalty than the general population. I'm sure you'll find plenty of private wealth and corporate power backing the American Civil Liberties Union.

Since those are aspects of the social order from which they gain, they tend to support them. By these criteria, the people who dominate the country tend to be liberal, and that reflects itself in an institution like PBS.

You've been on NPR just twice in 23 years, and on The MacNeil-Lehrer News Hour *once in its almost 20 years. What if you'd been on* MacNeil-Lehrer *ten times? Would it make a difference?*

Not a lot. By the way, I'm not quite sure of those numbers; my own memory isn't that precise. I've been on local PBS stations in particular towns.

I'm talking about the national network.

Then probably something roughly like those numbers is correct. But it wouldn't make a lot of difference.

In fact, in my view, if the managers of the propaganda system were more intelligent, they'd allow more leeway to real dissidents and critics. That would give the impression of broader debate and discussion and hence would have a legitimizing function, but it still wouldn't make much of a dent, given the overwhelming weight of propaganda on the other side. By the way, that propaganda system includes not just how issues are framed in news stories but also how they're presented in entertainment programming— that huge area of the media that's simply devoted to diverting people and making them more stupid and passive.

That's not to say I'm against opening up these media a bit, but I would think it would have a limited effect. What you need is something that presents every day, in a clear and comprehensive fashion, a different picture of the world, one that reflects the concerns and interests of ordinary people, and that takes something like the point of view with regard to democracy and participation that you find in people like Jefferson or Dewey.

Where that happens—and it has happened, even in modern societies—it has effects. In England, for example, you did have major mass media of this kind up until the 1960s, and it helped sustain and enliven a working class culture. It had a big effect on British society.

What do you think about the Internet?

I think that there are good things about it, but there are also aspects of it that concern and worry me. This is an intuitive response—I can't prove it—but my feeling is that, since people aren't Martians or robots, direct face-to-face contact is an extremely important part of human life. It helps develop self-understanding and the growth of a healthy personality.

You just have a different relationship to somebody when you're looking at them than you do when you're punching away at a keyboard and some symbols come back. I suspect that extending that form of abstract and remote relationship, instead of direct, personal contact, is going to have unpleasant effects on what people are like. It will diminish their humanity, I think.

Sports

In 1990, in one of our many interviews, we had a brief discussion about the role and function of sports in American society, part of which was subsequently excerpted in *Harper's.* I've probably gotten more comments about that than anything else I've ever recorded. You really pushed some buttons.

I got some funny reactions, a lot of irate reactions, as if I were somehow taking people's fun away from them. I have nothing against sports. I like to watch a good basketball game and that sort of thing. On the other hand, we have to recognize that the mass hysteria about spectator sports plays a significant role.

First of all, spectator sports make people more passive, because you're not doing them—you're watching somebody doing them. Secondly, they engender jingoist and chauvinist attitudes, sometimes to quite an extreme degree.

I saw something in the newspapers just a day or two ago about how high school teams are now so antagonistic and passionately committed to winning at all costs that they had to abandon the standard handshake before or after the game. These kids can't even do civil things like greeting one another because they're ready to kill one another.

It's spectator sports that engender those attitudes, particularly when they're designed to organize a community to be hysterically committed to their gladiators. That's very dangerous, and it has lots of deleterious effects.

I was reading something about the glories of the information superhighway not too long ago. I can't quote it exactly, but it was talking about how wonderful and empowering these new interactive technologies are going to be. Two basic examples were given.

For women, interactive technologies are going to offer highly improved methods of home shopping. So you'll be able to watch the tube and some model will appear with a product and you're supposed to think, God, I've got to have that. So you press a button and they deliver it to your door within a couple of hours. That's how interactive technology is supposed to liberate women.

For men, the example involved the Super Bowl. Every red-blooded American male is glued to it. Today, all they can do is watch it and cheer and drink beer, but the new interactive technology will let them actually participate in it. While the quarterback is in the huddle calling the next play, the people watching will be able to decide what the play should be.

If they think he should pass, or run, or punt, or whatever, they'll be able to punch that into their computer and their vote will be recorded. It won't have any effect on what the quarterback does, of course, but after the play the television channel will be able to put up the numbers—63% said he should have passed, 24% said he should have run, etc.

That's interactive technology for men. Now you're really participating in the world. Forget about all this business of deciding what ought to happen with health care—now you're doing something really important.

This scenario for interactive technology reflects an understanding of the stupefying effect spectator sports have in making people passive, atomized, obedient nonpartici-pants—nonquestioning, easily controlled and easily disciplined.

At the same time, athletes are lionized or—in the case of Tonya Harding, say—demonized.

If you can personalize events of the world—whether it's Hillary Clinton or Tonya Harding—you've succeeded in directing people away from what really matters and is important. The John F. Kennedy cult is a good example, with the effects it's had on the left.

Religious fundamentalism

In his book *When Time Shall Be No More,* historian Paul Boyer states that, "surveys show that from one third to one half of [all Americans] believe that the future can be interpreted from biblical prophecies." I find this absolutely stunning.

I haven't seen that particular number, but I've seen plenty of things like it. I saw a cross-cultural study a couple of years ago—I think it was published in England—that compared a whole range of societies in terms of beliefs of that kind. The US stood out— it was unique in the industrial world. In fact, the measures for the US were similar to pre-industrial societies.

Why is that?

That's an interesting question. This is a very fundamentalist society. It's like Iran in its degree of fanatic religious commitment. For example, I think about 75% of the US population has a literal belief in the devil.

There was a poll several years ago on evolution. People were asked their opinion on various theories of how the world of living creatures came to be what it is. The number of people who believed in Darwinian evolution was less than 10%. About half the population believed in a church doctrine of divine-guided evolution. Most of the rest presumably believed that the world was created a couple of thousand years ago.

These are very unusual results. Why the US should be off the spectrum on these issues has been discussed and debated for some time.

I remember reading something maybe ten or fifteen years ago by a political scientist who writes about these things, Walter Dean Burnham. He suggested that this may be a reflection of depoliticization—that is, the inability to participate in a meaningful fashion in the political arena may have a rather important psychic effect.

That's not impossible. People will find some ways of identifying themselves, becoming associated with others, taking part in something. They're going to do it some way or other. If they don't have the option to participate in labor unions, or in political organizations that actually function, they'll find other ways. Religious fundamentalism is a classic example.

We see that happening in other parts of the world right now. The rise of what's called

Islamic fundamentalism is, to a significant extent, a result of the collapse of secular nationalist alternatives that were either discredited internally or destroyed.

In the nineteenth century, you even had some conscious efforts on the part of business leaders to promote fire-and-brimstone preachers who led people to look at society in a more passive way. The same thing happened in the early part of the industrial revolution in England. E.P. Thompson writes about it in his classic, *The Making of the English Working Class.*

In a State of the Union speech, Clinton said, "We can't renew our country unless more of us—I mean, all of us—are willing to join churches." What do you make of this?

I don't know exactly what was in his mind, but the ideology is very straightforward. If people devote themselves to activities that are out of the public arena, then we folks in power will be able to run things the way we want.

Don't tread on me

I'm not quite clear about how to formulate this question. It has to do with the nature of US society as exemplified in comments like *do your own thing, go it alone, don't tread on me, the pioneer spirit*—all that deeply individualistic stuff. What does that tell you about American society and culture?

It tells you that the propaganda system is working full-time, because there is no such ideology in the US. Business certainly doesn't believe it. All the way back to the origins of American society, business has insisted on a powerful, interventionist state to support its interests, and it still does.

There's nothing individualistic about corporations. They're big conglomerate institutions, essentially totalitarian in character. Within them, you're a cog in a big machine. There are few institutions in human society that have such strict hierarchy and top-down control as a business organization. It's hardly *don't tread on me*—you're being tread on all the time.

The point of the ideology is to prevent people who are outside the sectors of coordinated power from associating with each other and entering into decision-making in the political arena. The point is to leave the powerful sectors highly integrated and organized, while atomizing everyone else.

That aside, there is another factor. There's a streak of independence and individuality in American culture that I think is a very good thing. This *don't tread on me* feeling is in many respects a healthy one—up to the point where it keeps you from working together with other people.

So it's got a healthy side and a negative side. Naturally it's the negative side that's emphasized in the propaganda and indoctrination.

The world

Toward greater inequality

In his column in the *New York Times,* Anthony Lewis wrote, "Since World War II, the world has experienced extraordinary growth." Meanwhile, at a meeting in Quito, Ecuador, Juan de Dias Parra, the head of the Latin American Association for Human Rights, said, "In Latin America today, there are 7 million more hungry people, 30 million more illiterate people, 10 million more families without homes, 40 million more unemployed persons than there were 20 years ago. There are 240 million human beings in Latin America without the necessities of life, and this when the region is richer and more stable than ever, according to the way the world sees it." How do you reconcile those two statements?

It just depends on which people you're talking about. The World Bank came out with a study on Latin America which warned that Latin America was facing chaos because of the extraordinarily high level of inequality, which is the highest in the world (and that's after a period of substantial growth). Even the things the World Bank cares about are threatened.

The inequality didn't just come from the heavens. There was a struggle over the course of Latin American development back in the mid-1940s, when the new world order of that day was being crafted.

The State Department documents on this are quite interesting. They said that Latin America was swept by what they called the "philosophy of the new nationalism," which called for increasing production for domestic needs and reducing inequality. The basic principle of this new nationalism was that the people of the country should be the prime beneficiary of the country's resources.

The US was sharply opposed to that and came out with an economic charter for the Americas that called for eliminating economic nationalism (as it's also called) in all of its forms and insisting that Latin American development be "complementary" to US development. That means we'll have the advanced industry and the technology and the peons in Latin America will produce export crops and do some simple operations that they can manage. But they won't develop economically the way we did.

Given the distribution of power, the US of course won. In countries like Brazil, we just took over—Brazil has been almost completely directed by American technocrats for about fifty years. Its enormous resources should make it one of the richest countries in the world, and it's had one of the highest growth rates. But thanks to our influence on Brazil's social and economic system, it's ranked around Albania and Paraguay in quality of life measures, infant mortality and so on.

It's true, as Lewis says, that there's been very substantial growth in the world. At the same time, there's incredible poverty and misery, and that's increased even more.

If you compare the percentage of world income held by the richest 20% and the poorest 20%, the gap has dramatically increased over the past thirty years. Comparing rich countries to poor countries, it's about doubled. Comparing rich people to poor people within countries, it's increased far more and is much sharper. That's the consequence of a particular kind of growth.

Do you think this trend of growth rates and poverty rates increasing simultaneously will continue?

Actually, growth rates have been slowing down a lot; in the past twenty years, they've been roughly half of what they were in the preceding twenty years. This tendency toward lower growth will probably continue.

One cause is the enormous increase in the amount of unregulated, speculative capital. The figures are really astonishing. John Eatwell, one of the leading specialists in finance at Cambridge University, estimates that, in 1970, about 90% of international capital was used for trade and long-term investment—more or less productive things—and 10% for speculation. By 1990, those figures had reversed: 90% for speculation and 10% for trade and long-term investment.

Not only has there been radical change in the nature of unregulated financial capital, but the quantity has grown enormously. According to a recent World Bank estimate, $14 *trillion* is now moving around the world, about $1 trillion or so of which moves every *day*.

This huge amount of mostly speculative capital creates pressures for deflationary policies, because what speculative capital wants is low growth and low inflation. It's driving much of the world into a low-growth, low-wage equilibrium.

This is a tremendous attack against government efforts to stimulate the economy. Even in the richer societies, it's very difficult; in the poorer societies, it's hopeless. What happened with Clinton's trivial stimulus package was a good indication. It amounted to nothing—$19 billion, but it was shot down instantly.

In the fall of 1993, the *Financial Times* [of London] trumpeted, "the public sector is in retreat everywhere." Is that true?

It's largely true, but major parts of the public sector are alive and well—in particular those parts that cater to the interests of the wealthy and the powerful. They're declining somewhat, but they're still very lively, and they're not going to disappear.

These developments have been going on for about twenty years now. They had to do with major changes in the international economy that became more or less crystallized by the early 1970s.

For one thing, US economic hegemony over the world had pretty much ended by then, and Europe and Japan had reemerged as major economic and political powers. The costs of the Vietnam War were very significant for the US economy, and extremely beneficial for its rivals. That tended to shift the world balance.

In any event, by the early 1970s, the US felt that it could no longer sustain its traditional role as—essentially—international banker. (This role was codified in the Bretton Woods agreements at the end of the Second World War, in which currencies were regulated relative to one another, and in which the de facto international currency, the US dollar, was fixed to gold.)

Nixon dismantled the Bretton Woods system around 1970. That led to tremendous growth in unregulated financial capital. That growth was rapidly accelerated by the short-term rise in the price of commodities like oil, which led to a huge flow of petrodollars into the international system. Furthermore, the telecommunications revolution made it extremely easy to transfer capital—or, rather, the electronic equivalent of capital—from one place to another.

There's also been a very substantial growth in the internationalization of production. It's now a lot easier than it was to shift production to foreign countries—generally highly repressive ones—where you get much cheaper labor. So a corporate executive who lives in Greenwich, Connecticut and whose corporate and bank headquarters are in New York City can have a factory somewhere in the Third World. The actual banking operations can take place in various offshore regions where you don't have to worry about supervision—you can launder drug money or whatever you feel like doing. This has led to a totally different economy.

With the pressure on corporate profits that began in the early 1970s, a big attack was launched on the whole social contract that had developed through a century of struggle and that had been more or less codified around the end of the Second World War with the New Deal and the European social welfare states. The attack was led by the US and England, and by now has reached continental Europe.

It's led to a serious decline in unionization, which carries with it a decline in wages and other forms of protection, and to a very sharp polarization of the society, primarily in the US and Britain (but it's spreading).

Driving in to work this morning, I was listening to the BBC [the British Broadcasting Company, Britain's national broadcasting service]. They reported a new study that found that children living in workhouses a century ago had better nutritional standards than millions of poor children in Britain today.

That's one of the grand achievements of [former British Prime Minister Margaret] Thatcher's revolution. She succeeded in devastating British society and destroying large parts of British manufacturing capacity. England is now one of the poorest countries in Europe—not much above Spain and Portugal, and well below Italy.

The American achievement was rather similar. We're a much richer, more powerful country, so it isn't possible to achieve quite what Britain achieved. But the Reaganites succeeded in driving US wages down so far that we're now the second lowest of the major industrial countries, barely above Britain. Labor costs in Italy are about 20% higher than in the US, and in Germany they're maybe 60% higher.

Along with that goes a deterioration of the general social contract and a breakdown of the kind of public spending that benefits the less privileged. Needless to say, the kind of public spending that benefits the wealthy and the privileged—which is enormous—remains fairly stable.

"Free trade"

My local newspaper, the Boulder [Colorado] *Daily Camera,* which is part of the Knight-Ridder chain, ran a series of questions and answers about GATT [the General Agreement on Tariffs and Trade]. They answered the question, Who would benefit from a GATT agreement? by writing, "Consumers would be the big winners." Does that track with your understanding?

If they mean rich consumers—yes, they'll gain. But much of the population will see a decline in wages, both in rich countries and poor ones. Take a look at NAFTA [the North American Free Trade Agreement], where the analyses have already been done. The day after NAFTA passed, the *New York Times* had its first article on its expected impact in the New York region. (Its conclusions apply to GATT too.)

It was a very upbeat article. They talked about how wonderful NAFTA was going to be. They said that finance and services will be particularly big winners. Banks, investment firms, PR firms, corporate law firms will do just great. Some manufacturers will also benefit—for example, publishing and the chemical industry, which is highly capital-intensive, with not many workers to worry about.

Then they said, Well, there'll be some losers too: women, Hispanics, other minorities, and semi-skilled workers—in other words, about two-thirds of the work force. But everyone else will do fine.

Just as anyone who was paying attention knew, the purpose of NAFTA was to create an even smaller sector of highly privileged people—investors, professionals, managerial classes. (Bear in mind that this is a rich country, so this privileged sector, although smaller, still isn't tiny.) It will work fine for them, and the general population will suffer.

The prediction for Mexico is exactly the same. The leading financial journal in Mexico, which is very pro-NAFTA, estimated that Mexico would lose about 25% of its manufacturing capacity in the first few years and about 15% of its manufacturing labor force. In addition, cheap US agricultural exports are expected to drive several million people off the land. That's going to mean a substantial increase in the unemployed workforce in Mexico, which of course will drive down wages.

On top of that, union organizing is essentially impossible. Corporations can operate internationally, but unions can't—so there's no way for the work force to fight back against the internationalization of production. The net effect is expected to be a decline in wealth and income for most people in Mexico and for most people in the US.

The strongest NAFTA advocates point that out in the small print. My colleague at MIT, Paul Krugman, is a specialist in international trade and, interestingly, one of the economists who's done some of the theoretical work showing why free trade doesn't work. He was nevertheless an enthusiastic advocate of NAFTA—which is, I should stress, not a free trade agreement.

He agreed with the *Times* that unskilled workers—about 70% of the work force—would lose. The Clinton administration has various fantasies about retraining workers, but that would probably have very little impact. In any case, they're doing nothing about it.

The same thing is true of skilled white-collar workers. You can get software programmers in India who are very well trained at a fraction of the cost of Americans. Somebody involved in this business recently told me that Indian programmers are actually being brought to the US and put into what are kind of like slave labor camps and kept at Indian salaries—a fraction of American salaries—doing software development. So that kind of work can be farmed out just as easily.

The search for profit, when it's unconstrained and free from public control, will naturally try to repress people's lives as much as possible. The executives wouldn't be doing their jobs otherwise.

What accounted for all the opposition to NAFTA?

The original expectation was that NAFTA would just sail through. Nobody would even know what it was. So it was signed in secret. It was put on a fast track in Congress, meaning essentially no discussion. There was virtually no media coverage. Who was going to know about a complex trade agreement?

That didn't work, and there are a number of reasons why it didn't. For one thing, the labor movement got organized for once and made an issue of it. Then there was this sort of maverick third-party candidate, Ross Perot, who managed to make it a public issue. And it turned out that as soon as the public learned anything about NAFTA, they were pretty much opposed.

I followed the media coverage on this, which was extremely interesting. Usually the media try to keep their class loyalties more or less in the background—they try to pretend they don't have them. But on this issue, the bars were down. They went berserk, and toward the end, when it looked like NAFTA might not pass, they just turned into raving maniacs.

But despite this enormous media barrage and the government attack and huge amounts of corporate lobbying (which totally dwarfed all the other lobbying, of course), the level of opposition remained pretty stable. Roughly 60% or so of those who had an opinion remained opposed.

The same sort of media barrage influenced the Gore-Perot television debate. I didn't watch it, but friends who did thought Perot just wiped Gore off the map. But the media proclaimed that Gore won a massive victory.

In polls the next day, people were asked what they thought about the debate. The percentage who thought that Perot had been smashed was far higher than the percentage who'd seen the debate, which means that most people were being told what to think by the media, not coming to their own conclusions.

Incidentally, what was planned for NAFTA worked for GATT—there was virtually no public opposition to it, or even awareness of it. It was rammed through in secret, as intended.

What about the position people like us find ourselves in of being "against," of being "anti-," reactive rather than pro-active?

NAFTA's a good case, because very few NAFTA critics were opposed to any agreement. Virtually everyone—the labor movement, the Congressional Office of Technology Assessment (a major report that was suppressed) and other critics (including me)—was saying there'd be nothing wrong with *a* North American Free Trade Agreement, but not this one. It should be different, and here are the ways in which it should be different—in some detail. Even Perot had constructive proposals. But all that was suppressed.

What's left is the picture that, say, Anthony Lewis portrayed in the *Times:* jingoist fanatics screaming about NAFTA. Incidentally, what's called the left played the same game. James Galbraith is an economist at the University of Texas. He had an article in a sort of left-liberal journal, *World Policy Review,* in which he discussed an article in which I said the opposite of what he attributed to me (of course—but that's typical).

Galbraith said there's this jingoist left—nationalist fanatics—who don't want Mexican workers to improve their lives. Then he went on about how the Mexicans are in favor of NAFTA. (True, if by "Mexicans" you mean Mexican industrialists and executives and corporate lawyers, not Mexican workers and peasants.)

All the way from people like James Galbraith and Anthony Lewis to way over to the right, you had this very useful fabrication—that critics of NAFTA were reactive and negative and jingoist and against progress and just wanted to go back to old-time protectionism. When you have essentially total control of the information system, it's rather easy to convey that image. But it simply isn't true.

Anthony Lewis also wrote, "The engine for [the world's] growth has been...vastly increased...international trade." Do you agree?

His use of the word "trade," while conventional, is misleading. The latest figures available (from about ten years ago—they're probably higher now) show that about 30% or 40% of what's called "world trade" is actually internal transfers within a corporation. I believe that about 70% of Japanese exports to the US are intrafirm transfers of this sort.

So, for example, Ford Motor Company will have components manufactured here in the US and then ship them for assembly to a plant in Mexico where the workers get much lower wages and where Ford doesn't have to worry about pollution, unions and all that nonsense. Then they ship the assembled part back here.

About half of what are called US exports to Mexico are intrafirm transfers of this sort. They don't enter the Mexican market, and there's no meaningful sense in which they're exports to Mexico. Still, that's called "trade."

The corporations that do this are huge totalitarian institutions, and they aren't governed by market principles—in fact, they promote severe market distortions. For example, a US corporation that has an outlet in Puerto Rico may decide to take its profits in Puerto Rico, because of tax rebates. It shifts its prices around, using what's called "transfer pricing," so it doesn't seem to be making a profit here.

There are estimates of the scale of governmental operations that interfere with trade, but I know of no estimates of internal corporate interferences with market processes. They're no doubt vast in scale, and are sure to be extended by the trade agreements.

GATT and NAFTA ought to be called "investor rights agreements," not "free trade agreements." One of their main purposes is to extend the ability of corporations to carry out market-distorting operations internally.

So when people like [Clinton's National Security Advisor] Anthony Lake talk about enlarging market democracy, he's enlarging something, but it's not markets and it's not democracy.

Mexico (and South Central LA)

I found the mainstream media coverage of Mexico during the NAFTA debate somewhat uneven. The *New York Times* has allowed in a number of articles that official corruption was—and is—widespread in Mexico. In fact, in one editorial, they virtually conceded that Salinas stole the 1988 presidential election. Why did that information come out?

I think it's impossible to repress. Furthermore, there were scattered reports in the *Times* of popular protest against NAFTA. Tim Golden, their reporter in Mexico, had a story a couple of weeks before the vote, probably in early November [1993], in which he said that lots of Mexican workers were concerned that their wages would decline after NAFTA. Then came the punch line.

He said that that undercuts the position of people like Ross Perot and others who think that NAFTA is going to harm American workers for the benefit of Mexican workers. In other words, the fact that they're *all* going to get screwed was presented as a critique of the people who were opposing NAFTA here!

There was very little discussion here of the large-scale popular protest in Mexico, which included, for example, the largest non-governmental trade union. (The main trade union is about as independent as the Soviet trade unions were, but there are some independent ones, and they were opposed to the agreement.)

The environmental movements and most of the other popular movements were opposed. The Mexican Bishops' Conference strongly endorsed the position the Latin American bishops took when they met at Santa Domingo [in the Dominican Republic] in December 1992.

That meeting in Santa Domingo was the first major conference of Latin American bishops since the ones at Puebla [Mexico] and Medellín [Colombia] back in the 1960s and 1970s. The Vatican tried to control it this time to make sure that they wouldn't come out with these perverse ideas about liberation theology and the preferential option for the poor. But despite a very firm Vatican hand, the bishops came out quite strongly against neoliberalism and structural adjustment and these free-market-for-the-poor policies. That wasn't reported here, to my knowledge.

There's been significant union-busting in Mexico.

Ford and VW are two big examples. A few years ago, Ford simply fired its entire Mexican work force and would only rehire, at much lower wages, those who agreed not to join a union. Ford was backed in this by the always-ruling PRI [the Institutional Revolutionary Party, which has controlled Mexico since the 1920s].

VW's case was pretty much the same. They fired workers who supported an independent union and only rehired, at lower wages, those who agreed not to support it.

A few weeks after the NAFTA vote in the US, workers at a GE and Honeywell plant in Mexico were fired for union activities. I don't know what the final outcome will be, but that's exactly the purpose of things like NAFTA.

In early January [1994], you were asked by an editor at the *Washington Post* to submit an article on the New Year's Day uprising in Chiapas [a state at the southern tip of Mexico, next to Guatemala]. Was this the first time the *Post* had asked you to write something?

It was the first time ever. I was kind of surprised, since I'm never asked to write for a national newspaper. So I wrote the article—it was for the *Sunday Outlook* section—but it didn't appear.

Was there an explanation?

No. It went to press, as far as I know. The editor who commissioned it called me, apparently after the deadline, to say that it looked OK to him but that it had simply been cancelled at some higher level. I don't know any more about it than that.

But I can guess. The article was about Chiapas, but it was also about NAFTA, and I think the *Washington Post* has been even more extreme than the *Times* in refusing to allow any discussion of that topic.

What happened in Chiapas doesn't come as very much of a surprise. At first, the government thought they'd just destroy the rebellion with tremendous violence, but then they backed off and decided to do it by more subtle violence, when nobody was looking. Part of the reason they backed off is surely their fear that there was just too much sympathy all over Mexico; if they were too up front about suppression, they'd cause themselves a lot of problems, all the way up to the US border.

The Mayan Indians in Chiapas are in many ways the most oppressed people in Mexico. Nevertheless, their problems are shared by a large majority of the Mexican population. This decade of neoliberal reforms has led to very little economic progress in Mexico but has sharply polarized the society. Labor's share in income has declined radically. The number of billionaires has shot up.

In that unpublished *Post* article, you wrote that the protest of the Indian peasants in Chiapas gives "only a bare glimpse of time bombs waiting to explode, not only in Mexico." What did you have in mind?

Take South Central Los Angeles, for example. In many respects, they are different societies, of course, but there are points of similarity to the Chiapas rebellion. South Central LA is a place where people once had jobs and lives, and those have been destroyed—in large part by the socio-economic processes we've been talking about.

For example, furniture factories went to Mexico, where they can pollute more cheaply. Military industry has somewhat declined. People used to have jobs in the steel industry, and they don't any more. So they rebelled.

The Chiapas rebellion was quite different. It was much more organized, and much more constructive. That's the difference between an utterly demoralized society like South Central Los Angeles and one that still retains some sort of integrity and community life.

When you look at consumption levels, doubtless the peasants in Chiapas are poorer than people in South Central LA. There are fewer television sets per capita. But by other, more significant criteria—like social cohesion—Chiapas is considerably more advanced. In the US, we've succeeded not only in polarizing communities but also in destroying their structures. That's why you have such rampant violence.

Haiti

Let's stay in Latin America and the Caribbean, which [former US Secretary of War and of State] Henry Stimson called "our little region over here which has never bothered anyone." Jean-Bertrand Aristide was elected president of Haiti in what's been widely described as a free and democratic election. Would you comment on what's happened since?

When Aristide won in December 1990 (he took office in February, 1991), it was a big surprise. He was swept into power by a network of popular grassroots organizations, what was called *Lavalas*—the flood—which outside observers just weren't aware of (since they don't pay attention to what happens among poor people). There had been very extensive and very successful organizing, and out of nowhere came this massive popular organization that managed to sweep their candidate into power.

The US was willing to support a democratic election, figuring that its candidate, a former World Bank official named Marc Bazin, would easily win. He had all the resources and support, and it looked like a shoe-in. He ended up getting 14% of the vote, and Aristide got about 67%.

The only question in the mind of anybody who knows a little history should have been, How is the US going to get rid of Aristide? The disaster became even worse in the first seven months of Aristide's office. There were some really amazing developments.

Haiti is, of course, an extremely impoverished country, with awful conditions. Aristide was nevertheless beginning to get places. He was able to reduce corruption extensively, and to trim a highly bloated state bureaucracy. He won a lot of international praise for this, even from the international lending institutions, which were offering him loans and preferential terms because they liked what he was doing.

Furthermore, he cut back on drug trafficking. The flow of refugees to the US virtually stopped. Atrocities were reduced to way below what they had been or would become. There was a considerable degree of popular engagement in what was going on, although the contradictions were already beginning to show up, and there were constraints on what he could do.

All of this made Aristide even more unacceptable from the US point of view, and we tried to undermine him through what were called—naturally—"democracy-enhancing programs." The US, which had never cared at all about centralization of power in Haiti when its own favored dictators were in charge, all of a sudden began setting up alternative institutions that aimed at undermining executive power, supposedly in the interests of greater democracy. A number of these alleged human rights and labor groups became the governing authorities after the coup, which came on September 30, 1991.

In response to the coup, the Organization of American States declared an embargo of Haiti; the US joined it, but with obvious reluctance. The Bush administration focused attention on Aristide's alleged atrocities and undemocratic activities, downplaying the major atrocities which took place right after the coup. The media went along with Bush's line, of course. While people were getting slaughtered in the streets of Port-au-Prince [Haiti's capital], the media concentrated on alleged human rights abuses under the Aristide government.

Refugees started fleeing again, because the situation was deteriorating so rapidly. The Bush administration blocked them—instituted a blockade, in effect—to send them back. Within a couple of months, the Bush administration had already undermined the embargo by allowing a minor exception—US-owned companies would be permitted to ignore it. The *New York Times* called that "fine-tuning" the embargo to improve the restoration of democracy!

Meanwhile, the US, which is known to be able to exert pressure when it feels like it, found no way to influence anyone else to observe the embargo, including the Dominican Republic next door. The whole thing was mostly a farce. Pretty soon Marc Bazin, the US candidate, was in power as prime minister, with the ruling generals behind him. That year—1992—US trade with Haiti was not very much below the norm, despite the so-called embargo (Commerce Department figures showed that, but I don't think the press ever reported it).

During the 1992 campaign, Clinton bitterly attacked the Bush administration for its inhuman policy of returning refugees to this torture chamber—which is, incidentally, a flat violation of the Universal Declaration of Human Rights, which we claim to uphold. Clinton claimed he was going to change all that, but his first act after being elected, even before he took office, was to impose even harsher measures to force fleeing refugees back into this hellhole.

Ever since then, it's simply been a matter of seeing what kind of finessing will be carried out to ensure that Haiti's popularly elected government doesn't come back into office. It doesn't have much longer to run [the next elections are scheduled for December, 1995], so the US has more or less won that game.

Meanwhile, the terror and atrocities increase. The popular organizations are getting decimated. Although the so-called embargo is still in place, US trade continues and, in fact, went up about 50% under Clinton. Haiti, a starving island, is exporting food to the US—about 35 times as much under Clinton as it did under Bush.

Baseballs are coming along nicely. They're produced in US-owned factories where the women who make them get 10¢ an hour—if they meet their quota. Since meeting the quota is virtually impossible, they actually make something like 5¢ an hour.

Softballs from Haiti are advertised in the US as being unusually good because they're hand-dipped into some chemical that makes them hang together properly. The ads don't mention that the chemical the women hand-dip the balls into is toxic and that, as a result, the women don't last very long at this work.

In his exile, Aristide has been asked to make concessions to the military junta.

And to the right-wing business community.

That's kind of curious. For the victim—the aggrieved party—to make concessions to his victimizer.

It's perfectly understandable. The Aristide government had entirely the wrong base of support. The US has tried for a long time to get him to "broaden his government in the interests of democracy."

This means throw out the two-thirds of the population that voted for him and bring in what are called "moderate" elements of the business community—the local owners or managers of those textile and baseball-producing plants, and those who are linked up with US agribusiness. When they're not in power, it's not democratic.

(The extremist elements of the business community think you ought to just slaughter everybody and cut them to pieces and hack off their faces and leave them in ditches. The moderates think you ought to have them working in your assembly plants for 14¢ an hour under indescribable conditions.)

Bring the moderates in and give them power and then we'll have a real democracy. Unfortunately, Aristide—being kind of backward and disruptive—has not been willing to go along with that.

Clinton's policy has gotten so cynical and outrageous that he's lost almost all major domestic support on it. Even the mainstream press is denouncing him at this point. So there will have to be some cosmetic changes made.

But unless there's an awful lot of popular pressure, our policies will continue and pretty soon we'll have the "moderates" in power.

Let's say Aristide is "restored." Given the destruction of popular organizations and the devastation of civil society, what are his and the country's prospects?

Some of the closest observation of this has been done by Americas Watch [a US-based human-rights monitoring organization]. They gave an answer to that question that I thought was plausible. In early 1993, they said that things were reaching the point that even if Aristide were restored, the lively, vibrant civil society based on grassroots organizations that had brought him to power would have been so decimated that it's unlikely that he'd have the popular support to do anything anyway.

I don't know if that's true or not. Nobody knows, any more than anyone knew how powerful those groups were in the first place. Human beings have reserves of courage that are often hard to imagine. But I think that's the plan—to decimate the organizations, to intimidate people so much that it won't matter if you have democratic elections.

There was an interesting conference run by the Jesuits in El Salvador several months before the Salvadoran elections; its final report came out in January [1994]. They were talking about the buildup to the elections and the ongoing terror, which was substantial. They said that the long-term effect of terror—something they've had plenty of experience with—is to domesticate people's aspirations, to make them think there's no alternative, to drive out any hope. Once you've done that, you can have elections without too much fear.

If people are sufficiently intimidated, if the popular organizations are sufficiently destroyed, if the people have had it beaten into their heads that either they accept the rule of those with the guns or else they live and die in unrelieved misery, then your elections will all come out the way you want. And everybody will cheer.

Cuban refugees are considered political and are accepted immediately into the US, while Haitian refugees are termed economic and are refused entry.

If you look at the records, many Haitians who are refused asylum in the US because they aren't considered to be political refugees are found a few days later hacked to pieces in the streets of Haiti.

There were a couple of interesting leaks from the INS [the Immigration and Naturalization Service]. One was from an INS officer who'd been working in our embassy in Port-au-Prince. In an interview with Dennis Bernstein of KPFA [a listener-supported radio station in Berkeley CA], he described in detail how they weren't even making the most perfunctory efforts to check the credentials of people who were applying for political asylum.

At about the same time, a document was leaked from the US interests section in Havana (which reviews applications for asylum in the US) in which they complain that they can't find genuine political asylum cases. The applicants they get can't really claim any serious persecution. At most they claim various kinds of harassment, which aren't enough to qualify them. So—there are the two cases, side by side.

I should mention that the US Justice Department has just made a slight change in US law which makes our violation of international law and the Universal Declaration of Human Rights even more grotesque. Now Haitian refugees who, by some miracle, reach US territorial waters can be shipped back. That's never been allowed before. I doubt that many other countries allow that.

Nicaragua

You recall the uproar in the 1980s about how the Sandinistas were abusing the Miskito Indians on Nicaragua's Atlantic coast. President Reagan, in his inimitable, understated style, said it was "a campaign of virtual genocide." UN Ambassador Jeane Kirkpatrick was a bit more restrained; she called it the "most massive human rights violation in Central America." What's happening now with the Miskitos?

Reagan and Kirkpatrick were talking about an incident in which, according to Americas Watch, several dozen Miskitos were killed and a lot of people were forcefully moved in a rather ugly way in the course of the contra war. The US terrorist forces were moving into the area and this was the Sandinista's reaction.

It was certainly an atrocity, but it's not even visible compared to the ones Jeane Kirkpatrick was celebrating in the neighboring countries at the time—and in Nicaragua, where the overwhelming mass of the atrocities were committed by the so-called "freedom fighters."

What's happening to the Miskitos now? When I was in Nicaragua in October 1993, church sources—the Christian Evangelical Church, primarily, which works in the Atlantic coast—were reporting that 100,000 Miskitos were starving to death as a result of the policies we were imposing on Nicaragua. Not a word about it in the media here. (More recently, it did get some slight reporting.)

People here are worrying about the fact that one typical consequence of US victories in the Third World is that the countries where we win immediately become big centers for drug flow. There are good reasons for that—it's part of the market system we impose on them.

Nicaragua has become a major drug transshipment center. A lot of the drugs go through the Atlantic coast, now that Nicaragua's whole governmental system has collapsed. Drug transhipment areas usually breed major drug epidemics, and there's one among the Miskitos, primarily among the men who dive for lobsters and other shellfish.

Both in Nicaragua and Honduras, these Miskito Indian divers are compelled by economic circumstances to do very deep diving without equipment. Their brains get smashed and they quickly die. In order to try to maintain their work rate, the divers stuff themselves with cocaine. It helps them bear the pain.

There's concern about drugs here, so *that* story got into the press. But of course nobody cares much about the working conditions. After all, it's a standard free-market technique. You've got plenty of superfluous people, so you make them work under horrendous conditions; when they die, you just bring in others.

China

Let's talk about human rights in one of our major trading partners—China.

During the Asia Pacific summit in Seattle [in November, 1993], Clinton announced that we'd be sending more high-tech equipment to China. This was in violation of a ban that was imposed to punish China for its involvement in nuclear and missile proliferation. The executive branch decided to "reinterpret" the ban, so we could send China nuclear generators, sophisticated satellites and supercomputers.

Right in the midst of that summit, a little tiny report appeared in the papers. In booming Kwangdong province, the economic miracle of China, 81 women were burned to death because they were locked into a factory. A couple of weeks later, 60 workers were killed in a Hong Kong-owned factory. China's Labor Ministry reported that 11,000 workers had been killed in industrial accidents just in the first eight months of 1993—twice as many as in the preceding year.

These sort of practices never enter the human rights debate, but there's been a big hullabaloo about the use of prison labor— front-page stories in the *Times*. What's the difference? Very simple. Because prison labor is state enterprise, it doesn't contribute to private profit. In fact, it undermines private profit, because it competes with private industry. But locking women into factories where they burn to death contributes to private profit.

So prison labor is a human rights violation, but there's no right not to be burned to death. We have to maximize profit. From that principle, everything follows.

Russia

Radio listener: I'd like to ask about US support for Yeltsin vs. democracy in Russia.

Yeltsin was the tough, autocratic Communist Party boss of Sverdlovsk. He's filled his administration with the old party hacks who ran things for him under the earlier Soviet system. The West likes him a lot because he's ruthless and because he's willing to ram through what are called "reforms" (a nice-sounding word).

These "reforms" are designed to return the former Soviet Union to the Third World status it had for the five hundred years before the Bolshevik Revolution. The Cold War was largely about the demand that this huge region of the world once again become what it had been—an area of resources, markets and cheap labor for the West.

Yeltsin is leading the pack on pushing the "reforms." Therefore he's a "democrat." That's what we call a democrat anywhere in the world—someone who follows the Western business agenda.

Dead children and debt service

After you returned from a recent trip to Nicaragua, you told me it's becoming more difficult to tell the difference between economists and Nazi doctors. What did you mean by that?

There's a report from UNESCO (which I didn't see reported in the US media) that estimated the human cost of the "reforms" that aim to return Eastern Europe to its Third World status.

UNESCO estimates that about a half a million deaths a year in Russia since 1989 are the direct result of the reforms, caused by the collapse of health services, the increase in disease, the increase in malnutrition and so on. Killing half a million people a year— that's a fairly substantial achievement for reformers.

The figures are similar, but not quite as bad, in the rest of Eastern Europe. In the Third World, the numbers are fantastic. For example, another UNESCO report estimated that about half a million children in Africa die every year simply from debt service. Not from the whole array of reforms—just from interest on their countries' debts.

It's estimated that about eleven million children die every year from easily curable diseases, most of which could be overcome by treatments that cost a couple of cents. But the economists tell us that to do this would be interference with the market system.

There's nothing new about this. It's very reminiscent of the British economists who, during the Irish potato famine in the mid-nineteenth century, dictated that Ireland must export food to Britain—which it did right through the famine—and that it shouldn't be given food aid because that would violate the sacred principles of political economy. These policies always happen to have the curious property of benefiting the wealthy and harming the poor.

Historical background

How the Nazis won the war

In his book *Blowback,* Chris Simpson described Operation Paper Clip, which involved the importation of large numbers of known Nazi war criminals, rocket scientists, camp guards, etc.

There was also an operation involving the Vatican, the US State Department and British intelligence, which took some of the worst Nazi criminals and used them, at first in Europe. For example, Klaus Barbie, the butcher of Lyon [France], was taken over by US intelligence and put back to work.

Later, when this became an issue, some of his US supervisors didn't understand what the fuss was all about. After all, we'd moved in—we'd replaced the Germans. We needed a guy who would attack the left-wing resistance, and here was a specialist. That's what he'd been doing for the Nazis, so who better could we find to do exactly the same job for us?

When the Americans could no longer protect Barbie, they moved him over to the Vatican-run "ratline," where Croatian Nazi priests and others managed to spirit him off to Latin America. There he continued his career. He became a big drug lord and narco-trafficker, and was involved in a military coup in Bolivia—all with US support.

But Barbie was basically small potatoes. This was a big operation, involving many top Nazis. We managed to get Walter Rauff, the guy who created the gas chambers, off to Chile. Others went to fascist Spain.

General Reinhard Gehlen was the head of German military intelligence on the eastern front. That's where the real war crimes were. Now we're talking about Auschwitz and other death camps. Gehlen and his network of spies and terrorists were taken over quickly by American intelligence and returned to essentially the same roles.

If you look at the American army's counterinsurgency literature (a lot of which is now declassified), it begins with an analysis of the German experience in Europe, written with the cooperation of Nazi officers. Everything is described from the point of view of the Nazis—which techniques for controlling resistance worked, which ones didn't. With barely a change, that was transmuted into American counterinsurgency literature. (This is discussed at some length by Michael McClintock in *Instruments of Statecraft*, a very good book that I've never seen reviewed.)

The US left behind armies the Nazis had established in Eastern Europe, and continued to support them at least into the early 1950s. By then the Russians had penetrated American intelligence, so the air drops didn't work very well any more.

You've said that if a real post-World War II history were ever written, this would be the first chapter.

It would be a part of the first chapter. Recruiting Nazi war criminals and saving them is bad enough, but imitating their activities is worse. So the first chapter would primarily describe US—and some British—operations throughout the world that aimed to destroy the anti-fascist resistance and restore the traditional, essentially fascist, order to power. (I've also discussed this in an earlier book in this series, *What Uncle Sam Really Wants.*)

In Korea (where we ran the operation alone), restoring the traditional order meant killing about 100,000 people just in the late 1940s, before the Korean War began. In Greece, it meant destroying the peasant and worker base of the anti-Nazi resistance and restoring Nazi collaborators to power.

When British and then American troops moved into southern Italy, they simply reinstated the fascist order—the industrialists. But the big problem came when the troops got to the north, which the Italian resistance had already liberated. The place was functioning—

industry was running. We had to dismantle all of that and restore the old order.

Our big criticism of the resistance was that they were displacing the old owners in favor of workers' and community control. Britain and the US called this "arbitrary replacement" of the legitimate owners. The resistance was also giving jobs to more people than were strictly needed for the greatest economic efficiency (that is, for maximum profit-making). We called this "hiring excess workers."

In other words, the resistance was trying to democratize the workplace and to take care of the population. That was understandable, since many Italians were starving. But starving people were their problem—our problem was to eliminate the hiring of excess workers and the arbitrary dismissal of owners, which we did.

Next we worked on destroying the democratic process. The left was obviously going to win the elections; it had a lot of prestige from the resistance, and the traditional conservative order had been discredited. The US wouldn't tolerate that. At its first meeting, in 1947, the National Security Council decided to withhold food and use other sorts of pressure to undermine the election.

But what if the communists still won? In its first report, NSC 1, the council made plans for that contingency: the US would declare a national emergency, put the Sixth Fleet on alert in the Mediterranean and support paramilitary activities to overthrow the Italian government.

That's a pattern that's been relived over and over. If you look at France and Germany and Japan, you get pretty much the same story.

Nicaragua is another case. You strangle them, you starve them, and then you have an election and everybody talks about how wonderful democracy is.

The person who opened up this topic (as he did many others) was Gabriel Kolko, in his classic book *Politics of War* in 1968. It was mostly ignored, but it's a terrific piece of work. A lot of the documents weren't around then, but his picture turns out to be quite accurate.

Chile

Richard Nixon's death generated much fanfare. Henry Kissinger said in his eulogy: "The world is a better place, a safer place, because of Richard Nixon." I'm sure he was thinking of Laos, Cambodia and Vietnam. But let's focus on one place that wasn't mentioned in all the media hoopla—Chile—and see how it's a "better, safer place." In early September 1970, Salvador Allende was elected president of Chile in a democratic election. What were his politics?

He was basically a social democrat, very much of the European type. He was calling for minor redistribution of wealth, to help the poor. (Chile was a very inegalitarian society.) Allende was a doctor, and one of the things he did was to institute a free milk program for half a million very poor, malnourished children. He called for nationalization of major industries like copper mining, and for a policy of international independence—meaning that Chile wouldn't simply subordinate itself to the US, but would take more of an independent path.

Was the election he won free and democratic?

Not entirely, because there were major efforts to disrupt it, mainly by the US. It wasn't the first time the US had done that. For example, our government intervened massively to prevent Allende from winning the preceding election, in 1964. In fact, when the Church Committee investigated years later, they discovered that the US spent more money per capita to get the candidate it favored elected in Chile in 1964 than was spent by both candidates (Johnson and Goldwater) in the 1964 election in the US!

Similar measures were undertaken in 1970 to try to prevent a free and democratic election. There was a huge amount of black propaganda about how if Allende won, mothers would be sending their children off to Russia to become slaves—stuff like that. The US also threatened to destroy the economy, which it could—and did—do.

Nevertheless, Allende won. A few days after his victory, Nixon called in CIA Director Richard Helms, Kissinger and others for a meeting on Chile. Can you describe what happened?

As Helms reported in his notes, there were two points of view. The "soft line" was, in Nixon's words, to "make the economy scream." The "hard line" was simply to aim for a military coup.

Our ambassador to Chile, Edward Korry, who was a Kennedy liberal type, was given the job of implementing the "soft line." Here's how he described his task: "to do all within our power to condemn Chile and the Chileans to utmost deprivation and poverty." That was the soft line.

There was a massive destabilization and disinformation campaign. The CIA planted stories in *El Mercurio* [Chile's most prominent paper] and fomented labor unrest and strikes.

They really pulled out the stops on this one. Later, when the military coup finally came [in September, 1973] and the government was overthrown—and thousands of people were being imprisoned, tortured and slaughtered—the economic aid which had been cancelled immediately began to flow again. As a reward for the military junta's achievement in reversing Chilean democracy, the US gave massive support to the new government.

Our ambassador to Chile brought up the question of torture to Kissinger. Kissinger rebuked him sharply—saying something like, Don't give me any of those political science lectures. We don't care about torture—we care about important things. Then he explained what the important things were.

Kissinger said he was concerned that the success of social democracy in Chile would be contagious. It would infect southern Europe—southern Italy, for example—and would lead to the possible success of what was then called Eurocommunism (meaning that Communist parties would hook up with social democratic parties in a united front).

Actually, the Kremlin was just as much opposed to Eurocommunism as Kissinger was, but this gives you a very clear picture of what the domino theory is all about. Even

Kissinger, mad as he is, didn't believe that Chilean armies were going to descend on Rome. It wasn't going to be that kind of an influence. He was worried that successful economic development, where the economy produces benefits for the general population—not just profits for private corporations—would have a contagious effect.

In those comments, Kissinger revealed the basic story of US foreign policy for decades.

You see that pattern repeating itself in Nicaragua in the 1980s.

Everywhere. The same was true in Vietnam, in Cuba, in Guatemala, in Greece. That's always the worry—the threat of a good example.

Kissinger also said, again speaking about Chile, "I don't see why we should have to stand by and let a country go Communist due to the irresponsibility of its own people."

As the *Economist* put it, we should make sure that policy is insulated from politics. If people are irresponsible, they should just be cut out of the system.

In recent years, Chile's economic growth rate has been heralded in the press.

Chile's economy isn't doing badly, but it's based almost entirely on exports—fruit, copper and so on—and thus is very vulnerable to world markets.

There was a really funny pair of stories yesterday. The *New York Times* had one about how everyone in Chile is so happy and satisfied with the political system that nobody's paying much attention to the upcoming election.

But the London *Financial Times* (which is the world's most influential business paper, and hardly radical) took exactly the opposite tack. They cited polls that showed that 75% of the population was very "disgruntled" with the political system (which allows no options).

There is indeed apathy about the election, but that's a reflection of the breakdown of Chile's social structure. Chile was a very vibrant, lively, democratic society for many, many years—into the early 1970s. Then, through a reign of fascist terror, it was essentially depoliticized. The breakdown of social relations is pretty striking. People work alone, and just try to fend for themselves. The retreat into individualism and personal gain is the basis for the political apathy.

Nathaniel Nash wrote the *Times'* Chile story. He said that many Chileans have painful memories of Salvador Allende's fiery speeches, which led to the coup in which thousands of people were killed [including Allende]. Notice that they don't have painful memories of the torture, of the fascist terror—just of Allende's speeches as a popular candidate.

Cambodia

Would you talk a little about the notion of unworthy vs. worthy victims?

[NY Newsday columnist and former New York Times reporter] Sidney Schanberg wrote an oped piece in the *Boston Globe* in which he blasted Senator Kerry of Massachusetts for being two-faced because Kerry refused to concede that the Vietnamese have not been entirely forthcoming about American POWs. Nobody, according to Schanberg, is willing to tell the truth about this.

He says the government ought to finally have the honesty to say that it left Indochina without accounting for all the Americans. Of course, it wouldn't occur to him to suggest that the government should be honest enough to say that we killed a couple of million people and destroyed three countries and left them in total wreckage and have been strangling them ever since.

It's particularly striking that this is Sidney Schanberg, a person of utter depravity. He's regarded as the great conscience of the press because of his courage in exposing the crimes of our official enemies—namely, Pol Pot [leader of Cambodia's Khmer Rouge rebel army]. He also happened to be the main US reporter in Phnom Penh [Cambodia's capital] in 1973. This was at the peak of the US bombardment of inner Cambodia, when hundreds of thousands of people (according to the best estimates) were being killed and the society was being wiped out.

Nobody knows very much about the bombing campaign and its effects because people like Sidney Schanberg refused to cover it. It wouldn't have been hard for him to cover it. He wouldn't have to go trekking off into the jungle—he could walk across the street from his fancy hotel in Phnom Penh and talk to any of the hundreds of thousands of refugees who'd been driven from the countryside into the city.

I went through all of his reporting—it's reviewed in detail in *Manufacturing Consent*, my book with Edward Herman [currently editor of *Lies of Our Times*]. You'll find a few scattered sentences here and there about the bombing, but not a single interview with the refugees.

There is one American atrocity he did report (for about three days); *The Killing Fields*, the movie that's based on his story, opens by describing it. What's the one report? American planes hit the wrong village—a government village. That's an atrocity; that he covered. How about when they hit the right village? We don't care about that.

Incidentally, the United States' own record with POWs has been atrocious—not only in Vietnam, where it was monstrous, but in Korea, where it was even worse. And after WW II, we kept POWs illegally under confinement, as did the British.

World War II POWs

Other Losses, a Canadian book, alleges it was official US policy to withhold food from German prisoners in World War II. Many of them supposedly starved to death.

That's James Bacque's book. There's been a lot of controversy about the details, and I'm not sure what the facts of the matter are. On the other hand, there are things about which there's no controversy. Ed Herman and I wrote about them back in the late 1970s.

Basically, the Americans ran what were called "re-education camps" for German POWs (the name was ultimately changed to something equally Orwellian). These camps were hailed as a tremendous example of our humanitarianism, because we were teaching the prisoners democratic ways (in other words, we were indoctrinating them into accepting our beliefs).

The prisoners were treated very brutally, starved, etc. Since these camps were in gross violation of international conventions, they were kept secret. We were afraid that the Germans might retaliate and treat American prisoners the same way.

Furthermore, the camps continued after the war; I forget for how long, but I think the US kept German POWs until mid-1946. They were used for forced labor, beaten and killed. It was even worse in England. They kept their German POWs until mid-1948. It was all totally illegal.

Finally, there was public reaction in Britain. The person who started it off was Peggy Duff, a marvelous woman who died a couple of years ago. She was later one of the leading figures in the CND [the Campaign for Nuclear Disarmament] and the international peace movement during the 1960s and 1970s, but she started off her career with a protest against the treatment of German POWs.

Incidentally, why only German POWs? What about the Italians? Germany's a very efficient country, so they've published volumes of documents on what happened to their POWs. But Italy's sort of laid back, so there was no research on their POWs. We don't know anything about them, although they were surely treated much worse.

When I was a kid, there was a POW camp right next to my high school. There were conflicts among the students over the issue of taunting the prisoners. The students couldn't physically attack the prisoners, because they were behind a barrier, but they threw things at them and taunted them. There were a group of us who thought this was horrifying and objected to it, but there weren't many.

Miscellaneous topics

Consumption vs. well-being

The United States, with 5% of the world's population, consumes 40% of the world's resources. You don't have to be a genius to figure out what that's leading to.

For one thing, a lot of that consumption is artificially induced—it doesn't have to do with people's real wants and needs. People would probably be better off and happier if they didn't have a lot of those things.

If you measure economic health by profits, then such consumption is healthy. If you measure the consumption by what it means to people, it's very unhealthy, particularly in the long term.

99

A huge amount of business propaganda—that is, the output of the public relations and advertising industry—is simply an effort to create wants. This has been well understood for a long time; in fact, it goes back to the early days of the Industrial Revolution.

For another thing, those who have more money tend to consume more, for obvious reasons. So consumption is skewed towards luxuries for the wealthy rather than towards necessities for the poor. That's true within the US and on a global scale as well. The richer countries are the higher consumers by a large measure, and within the richer countries, the wealthy are higher consumers by a large measure.

Cooperative enterprises

There's a social experiment in Mondragón in the Basque region of Spain. Can you describe it?

Mondragón is basically a very large worker-owned cooperative with many different industries in it, including some fairly sophisticated manufacturing. It's economically quite successful, but since it's inserted into a capitalist economy, it's no more committed to sustainable growth than any other part of the capitalist economy is.

Internally, it's not worker-controlled—it's manager-controlled. So it's a mixture of what's sometimes called industrial democracy—which means ownership, at least in principle, by the work force—along with elements of hierarchic domination and control (as opposed to worker management).

I mentioned earlier that businesses are about as close to strict totalitarian structures as any human institutions are. Something like Mondragón is considerably less so.

The coming eco-catastrophe

Radio listener: What's happening in the growing economies in Southeast Asia, China, etc.? Is it going to be another example of capitalist exploitation, or can we expect to see some kind of change in their awareness?

Right now, it's catastrophic. In countries like Thailand or China, ecological catastrophes are looming. These are countries where growth is being fueled by multinational investors for whom the environment is what's called an "externality" (which means you don't pay any attention to it). So if you destroy the forests in Thailand, say, that's OK as long as you make a short-term profit out of it.

In China, the disasters which lie not too far ahead could be extraordinary—simply because of the country's size. The same is true throughout Southeast Asia.

But when the environmental pressures become such that the very survival of people is jeopardized, do you see any change in the actions?

Not unless people react. If power is left in the hands of transnational investors, the people will just die.

Nuclear power

At a conference in Washington DC, a woman in the audience got up and decried the fact that you're in favor of nuclear power. Are you?

No. I don't think anybody's in favor of nuclear power, even business, because it's too expensive. But what I am in favor of is being rational on the topic. That means recognizing that the question of nuclear power isn't a moral one—it's a technical one. You have to ask what the consequences of nuclear power are, versus the alternatives.

There's a range of other alternatives, including conservation, solar and so on. Each has its own advantages and disadvantages. But imagine that the only alternatives were hydrocarbons and nuclear power. If you had to have one or the other, you'd have to ask yourself which is more dangerous to the environment, to human life, to human society. It's not an entirely simple question.

For example, suppose that fusion were a feasible alternative. It could turn out to be nonpolluting. But there are also negative factors. Any form of nuclear power involves quite serious problems of radioactive waste disposal, and can also contribute to nuclear weapons proliferation. Fusion would require a high degree of centralization of state power too.

On the other hand, the hydrocarbon industry, which is highly polluting, also promotes centralization. The energy corporations are some of the biggest in the world, and the

Pentagon system is constructed to a significant degree to maintain their power.

In other words, there are questions that have to be thought through. They're not simple.

The family

You've suggested that, to further democracy, people should be "seeking out authoritarian structures and challenging them, eliminating any form of absolute power and hierarchic power." How would that work in a family structure?

In any structure, including a family structure, there are various forms of authority. A patriarchal family may have very rigid authority, with the father setting rules that others adhere to, and in some cases even administering severe punishment if there's a violation of them.

There are other hierarchical relations among siblings, between the mother and father, gender relations, and so on. These all have to be questioned. Sometimes I think you'll find that there's a legitimate claim to authority—that is, the challenge to authority can sometimes be met. But the burden of proof is always on the authority.

So, for example, some form of control over children is justified. It's fair to prevent a child from putting his or her hand in the oven, say, or from running across the street in traffic. It's proper to place clear bounds on children. They want them—they want to understand where they are in the world.

However, all of these things have to be done with sensitivity and with self-aware-ness and with the recognition that any authoritarian role requires justification. It's never self-justifying.

When does a child get to the point where the parent doesn't need to provide authority?

I don't think there are formulas for this. For one thing, we don't have solid scientific knowledge and understanding of these things. A mixture of experience and intuition, plus a certain amount of study, yields a limit-ed framework of understanding (about which people may certainly differ). And there are also plenty of individual differences.

So I don't think there's a simple answer to that question. The growth of autonomy and self-control, and expansion of the range of legitimate choices, and the ability to exercise them—that's growing up.

=======

What you can do

Radio listener: Taking it down to the individual, per-sonal level, I got a notice in my public service bill that said they're asking for a rate hike. I work, and I really don't have the time to sit down and write a let-ter of protest. This happens all the time, and not just with me. Most people don't have time to be active politically to change something. So those rate hikes go through without anybody ever really pointing out what's going on. I've often wondered why there isn't a limitation on the amount of profit any business can make (I know this probably isn't democratic).

I think it's highly democratic. There's nothing in the principle of democracy that says that power and wealth should be so highly concentrated that democracy becomes a sham.

But your first point is quite correct. If you're a working person, you just don't have time—alone—to take on the power company. That's exactly what organization is about. That's exactly what unions are for, and political parties that are based on working people.

If such a party were around, they'd be the ones speaking up for you and telling the truth about what's going on with the rate hike. Then they'd be denounced by the Anthony Lewises of the world for being anti-democratic—in other words, for representing popular interests rather than power interests.

Radio listener: I'm afraid there may be a saturation point of despair just from knowing the heaviness of the truth that you impart. I'd like to strongly lobby you to begin devoting maybe 10% or 15% of your appearances or books or articles towards tangible, detailed things that people can do to try to change the world. I've heard a few occasions where someone asks you that question and your response is, Organize. Just do it.

I try to keep it in the back of my mind and think about it, but I'm afraid that the answer is always the same. There is only one way to deal with these things. Being alone, you can't do anything. All you can do is deplore the situation.

But if you join with other people, you can make changes. Millions of things are possible, depending on where you want to put your efforts.

To help you get started, Odonian Press has put together a list of 144 organizations that work to make the world a better place. It begins on the next page.

You may also find a couple of current books useful. Howard Zinn's *You Can't Be Neutral on a Moving Train* (Beacon, 1994) is well-written (as always) and has an optimistic message. Michael Albert's *Stop The Killing Train: Radical Visions for Radical Change* (South End, 1993) is also forward-looking and constructive.

Noam Chomsky

The organizations on this list were suggested by Noam Chomsky, Jane Maxwell, Chris Rosene, Davida Coady, Susan McCallister, Gar Smith, Sheila Katz, David Barsamian and myself. I've grouped them into the following categories:

- affordable housing
- anti-war, anti-military and economic conversion
- Canadian
- church groups
- civil rights
- communications and research (general)
- environmental
- funding
- general and miscellaneous
- health and reproductive rights
- human rights
- labor and community organizing
- Latin America
- Middle East
- political parties and groups
- Third World development
- women's issues

It's unlikely that any of us would agree with everyone else's choices, so please don't assail us with complaints about which organizations are—or aren't—included on the list. (Thanks.)

We all realize that there are *many, many* other worthwhile groups—particularly small, local ones. One way to find out about them is to ask any of the regional funding foundations on the list below for the names of the organizations they support.

Arthur Naiman

Affordable housing

Fund for an Open Society
311 S Juniper, #400
Philadelphia PA 19107
215 735 6915

Habitat for Humanity
121 Habitat St
Americus GA 31709
912 924 6935

South Shore Bank
7054 S Jeffery Blvd
Chicago IL 60649
312 288 1000

Anti-war, anti-military and economic conversion

Campaign for Peace and Democracy
Box 1640 Cathedral Station
New York NY 10025
212 666 5924

Center for Defense Information
1500 Massachusetts Ave NW
Washington DC 20005
202 862 0700

Center for Economic Conversion
222 View St
Mountain View CA 94041
415 968 8798

Central Committee for Conscientious Objectors
(Western Region)
655 Sutter, #514
San Francisco CA 94102
415 474 3002

Livermore Conversion Project
Box 31835
Oakland CA 94604
510 832 4347

Nevada Desert Experience
Box 4487
Las Vegas NV 89127
702 646 4814

PeaceNet *(online)*
see Institute for Global Communications *in the Communications section*

Veterans Speakers Alliance
942 Market St, #709
San Francisco CA 94102
415 255 7331

War Resisters League
339 Lafayette St
New York NY 10012
212 228 0450

Canadian
Also see Church groups.

Canadian Environmental Law Association
517 College St, #401
Toronto, Ontario
M6G 4A2 Canada
416 960 2284

CCIC (Canadian Council for International Cooperation)
1 Nicholas St, #300
Ottawa, Ontario
K1N 7B7 Canada
613 241 7007

CUSO
135, rue Rideau St
Ottawa, Ontario
K1N 9K7 Canada
613 241 1264

Oxfam Canada
294 Albert St, #300
Ottawa, Ontario
K1P6E6 Canada
613 237 5236

Church groups

**American Friends
  Service Committee**
1501 Cherry St
Philadelphia PA 19102
215 241 7000

**Anglican Church of
  Canada**
600 Jarvis St
Toronto, Ontario
M4Y 2J6 Canada
416 924 9192

**Canadian Catholic
  Organization for Devel-
  opment and Peace**
5633 Sherbrooke E
Montréal, Québec
H1N 1A3 Canada
514 257 8711

**Maryknoll Mission
  Association of the
  Faithful**
Box 307
Maryknoll NY10545
914 762 6364

**National Council of
  Churches**
475 Riverside Dr
New York NY 10115
212 870 2511

**Unitarian-Universalist
  Association**
78 Beacon St
Boston MA 02108
617 742 2100

United Church of Canada
85 St. Clair Ave E
Toronto, Ontario
M4T 1M8 Canada
416 925 5931

Civil rights

**American Civil Liberties
  Union**
132 W 43rd St
New York NY 10036
212 944 9800

Asian Law Caucus
468 Bush St, 3rd flr
San Francisco CA 94108
415 391 1655

**Center for Constitutional
  Rights**
666 Broadway
New York NY 10012
212 614 6464

Drug Policy Foundation
4455 Connecticut Ave
  NW, #B-500
Washington DC 20008
202 537 5005

MALDEF (Mexican-Amer-
  ican Legal Defense and
  Education Fund)
634 S Spring St
Los Angeles CA 90014
213 629 2512

NAACP (National Association for the Advancement of Colored People)
4805 Mount Hope Dr
Baltimore MD 21215
410 358 8900

National Gay and Lesbian Task Force
2320 17th St NW
Washington DC 20009
202 332 6483

National Emergency Civil Liberties Committee
175 Fifth Ave
New York NY 10010
212 673 2040

National Urban League
500 E 62nd St
New York NY 10021
212 310 9000

Native American Rights Fund
1506 Broadway
Boulder CO 80302
303 447 8760

NORML (National Organization for the Reform of Marijuana Laws)
1001 Connecticut Ave NW, #1010
Washington DC 20036
202 483 5500

Southern Poverty Law Center
Box 2087
Montgomery AL 36102
205 264 0286

Communications and research (general)

Also see the publishers listed on pp. 118–19.

Center for Investigative Reporting
568 Howard St, 5th flr
San Francisco 94105
415 543 1200

Covert Action
1500 Massachusetts Ave NW, #732
Washington DC 20005
202 331 9763

Data Center
464 19th St
Oakland CA 94612
510 835 4692

FAIR (Fairness and Accuracy in Reporting)
130 W 25th St
New York NY 10001
212 633 6700

Institute for Global Communications
18 Deboom St
San Francisco CA 94107
415 442 0220
mother organization to EcoNet, LaborNet and PeaceNet

Institute for Media Analysis
145 W 4th St
New York NY 10012
212 254 1061
publishes Lies of Our Times

Institute for Policy Studies
1601 Connecticut Ave NW, #500
Washington DC 20009
202 234 9382

KFCF
Box 4364
Fresno CA 93744
209 233 2221

KPFA
1929 Martin Luther King Jr. Way
Berkeley CA 94704
510 848 6767

KPFK
3729 Cahuenga Blvd W
North Hollywood CA 91604
818 985 2711

KPFT
419 Lovett
Houston TX 77006
713 526 4000

The Nation Institute
72 Fifth Ave
New York NY 10011
212 463 9270 or
212 242 8400

Pacifica National News
700 H St NW
Washington DC 20001
202 783 1620
mother organization to KFCF, KPFA, KPFK, KPFT, WBAI and WPSW

The Progressive
409 E Main St
Madison WI 53703
608 257 4626

Public Media Center
466 Green St, #300
San Francisco CA 94133
415 434 1403

WBAI
505 Eighth Ave, 19th flr
New York, NY 10018
212 279 0707

WPSW
702 H St NW
Washington DC 20001
202 783 3100

Z Media Institute
18 Millfield St
Woods Hole MA 02543
508 548 9063

Environmental
Also see Canadian *groups*

Alliance for a Paving Moratorium
Box 4347
Arcata CA 95521
707 826 7775

Earth First!
Box 1415
Eugene OR 97440
503 741 9191

Earth Island Institute
300 Broadway, #28
San Francisco CA 94133
415 788 3666

EcoNet *(online)*
see Institute for Global Communications *above*

Greenpeace
1436 U St NW
Washington DC 20009
202 462 1177

**Indigenous Environ-
mental Network**
Box 485
Bemidji MN 56601
218 751 4967

PEG (Political Ecology
Group)
519 Castro St, Box 111
San Francisco CA 94114
415 641 7835

**Student Environmental
Action Coalition**
Box 1168
Chapel Hill NC 27514
919 967 4600

Funding

*The first listing is a
national network office
for progressive funds.
The other listings are
member funds, all of
which (except Resist)
have a regional focus.*

Funding Exchange
666 Broadway, #500
New York NY 10012
212 529 5300

**Appalachian Community
Fund**
517 Union Ave, #206
Knoxville TN 37902
615 523 5783

**Bread and Roses
Community Fund**
1500 Walnut St, #1305
Philadelphia PA 19102
215 731 1107

Chinook Fund
2418 W 32nd Ave
Denver CO 80211
303 455 6905

Crossroads Fund
3411 W Diversey Ave,
#20
Chicago IL 60647
312 227 7676

**Fund for Southern
Communities**
552 Hill St SE
Atlanta GA 30312
404 577 3178

**Haymarket People's
Fund**
42 Seaverns Ave
Jamaica Plain MA 02130
617 522 7676

Headwaters Fund
122 W Franklin Ave,
#518
Minneapolis MN 55404
612 879 0602

Liberty Hill Foundation
1316 Third St
Promenade, #B-4
Santa Monica CA 90401
310 458 1450

**McKenzie River
Gathering Foundation**
3558 SE Hawthorne
Portland OR 97214
503 233 0271

North Star Fund
666 Broadway, 5th flr
New York NY 10012
212 460 5511

People's Fund
1325 Nuuanu Ave
Honolulu HI 96817
808 526 2441

Resist
One Summer St
Somerville MA 02143
617 623 5110

Three Rivers Community Fund
100 N Braddock Ave, #207
Pittsburgh PA 15208
412 243 9250

Vanguard Public Foundation
383 Rhode Island, #301
San Francisco CA 94103
415 487 2111

Wisconsin Community Fund
122 State St, #508
Madison WI 53703
608 251 6834

General and miscellaneous

Center for Ethics and Economic Policy
2512 9th St, #3
Berkeley CA 94710
510 549 9931

Center for Living Democracy
Rural Route 1
Black Fox Rd
Brattleboro VT 05301
802 254 1234

Davis-Putter Scholarship Fund
744 Broad St, #2500
Newark NJ 07102

Gray Panthers
2025 Pennsylvania Ave NW, #821
Washington DC 20006
202 466 3132

INFACT
256 Hanover St
Boston MA 02113
617 742 4583

Neighbor to Neighbor
2601 Mission, #400
San Francisco CA 94110
415 824 3355
also DC, 202 543 2429

People for the American Way
2000 M St NW, #400
Washington DC 20036
202 467 4999

Physicians for Social Responsibility
1101 14th St NW, #700
Washington DC 20036
202 898 0150

Public Citizen
2000 P St NW, #700
Washington DC 20036
202 833 3000

Quixote Center
Box 5206
Hyattsville MD 20782
301 699 0042

Rosenberg Fund for Children
1145 Main St, #408
Springfield MA 01103
413 739 9020

Women's International League for Peace and Freedom
1213 Race St
Philadelphia PA 19107
215 563 7110

Health and reproductive rights

Advocates for Youth
1025 Vermont Ave NW, #200
Washington DC 20005
202 347 5700

Coalition for the Medical Rights of Women
558 Capp St
San Francisco CA 94110
415 647 2694

Hesperian Foundation
2796 Middlefield Rd
Palo Alto CA 94306
415 325 9017

NARAL *(National Abortion Rights Action League)*
1156 15th St NW, #700
Washington DC 20005
202 828 9300

Partners in Health
113 River St
Cambridge MA 02139
617 661 4564

Planned Parenthood
810 Seventh Ave
New York NY 10019
212 541 7800

Seva Foundation
8 N San Pedro Rd
San Rafael CA 94903
415 492 1829

Human rights

Amnesty International USA
322 Eighth Ave
New York NY 10001
212 807 8400

Coalition for Immigrant and Refugee Rights and Services
995 Market St, #1108
San Francisco CA 94103
415 243 8215

East Timor Action Network
Box 1182
White Plains NY 10602
914 428 7299
also San Francisco, 415 387 2822, and Vancouver, 604 264 9973

Human Rights Watch
(includes Americas Watch, Africa Watch, Asia Watch, etc.)
485 Fifth Ave, 3rd flr
New York NY 10017
212 972 8400

Physicians for Human Rights
100 Boylston St, #702
Boston MA 02116
617 695 0041

Labor and community organizing

Center for Third World Organizing
1218 E 21st St
Oakland CA 94606
510 533 7583

Industrial Areas Foundation
36 New Hyde Park Road
Franklin Square NY 11010
516 354 1076

LaborNet *(online)*
see Institute for Global Communications *in the Communications section*

Labor Party Advocates
Box 53177
Washington DC 20009
202 319 1932

Latin America

Barricada International
Box 410150
San Francisco CA 94141
415 621 8981

CISPES (Committee in Solidarity with the People of El Salvador)
19 W 21st St, #502
New York NY 10010
212 229 1290

CHRICA (Committee for Health Rights in Central America)
347 Delores St , #210
San Francisco CA 94110
415 431 7760

Disarm/Cuban Medical Project
36 E 12th St
New York NY 10003
212 475 3232

Documentation Exchange
Box 2327
Austin TX 78768
512 476 9841

Global Exchange
2017 Mission, #303
San Francisco CA 94110
415 255 7296

GNIB (Guatemalan News and Information Bureau)
Box 28594
Oakland CA 94604
510 835 0810

Guatemala Partners
945 G St NW
Washington DC 20001
202 783 1123

Inter-Hemispheric Education Resource Center
Box 4506
Albuquerque NM 87196
505 842 8288

MADRE
121 W 27th St, #301
New York NY 10001
212 627 0444

NACLA (North American Congress on Latin America)
475 Riverside Dr, #454
New York NY 10115
212 870 3146

Nicaragua Network
1247 E St SE
Washington DC 20003
202 544 9355

NISGUA (Network in Solidarity with the People of Guatemala)
1500 Massachusetts Ave NW, #214
Washington DC 20005
202 483 0050

Office of the Americas
8124 W Third St, #202
Los Angeles CA 90048
213 852 9808

International Peace for Cuba Appeal
39 W 14th St, #206
New York NY 10011
212 633 6646
also San Francisco, 415 821 6545

Pueblo to People
2105 Silber Rd, #101
Houston TX 77055
713 956 1172

Resource Center of the Americas
317 17th Ave SE
Minneapolis MN 55404
612 627 9445

San Carlos Foundation
1065 Creston Road
Berkeley CA 94708
510 525 3787

Witness for Peace
2201 P St NW
Washington DC 20037
202 797 1160

WOLA (Washington Office on Latin America)
110 Maryland Ave NE, #404
Washington DC 20002
202 544 8045

Middle East

Jewish Peace Lobby
8604 Second Ave, #317
Silver Spring MD 20910
301 589 8764

Middle East Children's Alliance
905 Parker St
Berkeley CA 94710
510 548 0542

Middle East Justice Network
Box 495
Boston MA 02112
617 542 5056

Search for Justice and Equality in Palestine/Israel
Box 3452
Framingham MA 01701
508 877 2611

Political parties and groups

Democratic Socialists of America
180 Varick St, 12th flr
New York NY 10014
212 727 8610

Green Party USA
Box 30208
Kansas City MO 64112
816 931 9366

New Party
227 W 40th St, #1303
New York NY 10018
212 302 5053

Third World development

Also see Canadian groups

Food First (Institute for Food and Development Policy)
398 60th St
Oakland CA 94618
510 654 4400

Center for International Policy
1755 Massachusetts Ave NW, #312
Washington DC 200365
202 232 3317

Oxfam America
26 West St
Boston MA 02111
617 482 1211

Results
236 Massachusetts Ave NE, #300
Washington DC 20002
202 543 9340

World Neighbors
4127 NW 126th
Oklahoma City OK 73120
405 946 3333

Women's issues

Also see Health and reproductive rights

Coalition of Labor Union Women
1126 16th St NW
Washington DC 20036
202 466 4610

Connexions
Box 14431
Berkeley CA 94712
510 549 3505

Ms. Foundation
120 Wall St, 33rd flr
New York, NY 10005
212 742 2300

9to5, National Association of Working Women
238 W Wisconsin Ave, #700
Milwaukee WI 53203
414 274 0925

NOW (National Organization of Women) **Legal Defense and Education Fund**
99 Hudson St
New York NY 10013
212 925 6635

WOW (Wider Opportunities for Women)
815 15th St NW, #916
Washington DC 20005
202 638 3143

Other books
by Noam Chomsky

These two pages list Noam Chomsky's other political books in reverse chronological order (alphabetically within years). His books on linguistics aren't included unless they contain some political material; neither are shorter works or collections of essays by various authors. Addresses and phone numbers for the smaller publishers are given the first time they're mentioned.

World Orders Old and New. Columbia University Press, 1994.

Letters from Lexington: Reflections on Propaganda (letters). Common Courage (Box 702, Monroe ME 04951; 800 497 3207), 1993.

The Prosperous Few and the Restless Many (compiled from interviews with David Barsamian). Odonian Press (Box 32375, Tucson AZ 85751; 602 296 4056 or 800 REAL STORY), 1993.

Rethinking Camelot. South End Press (116 St Botolph St, Boston MA 02115; 617 266 0629 or 800 533 8478), 1993.

Year 501: The Conquest Continues. South End, 1993.

Chronicles of Dissent (interviews with David Barsamian). Common Courage (Box 702, Monroe ME 04951; 800 497 3207), 1992.

What Uncle Sam Really Wants (compiled from talks and interviews). Odonian, 1992.

Deterring Democracy. Verso (29 W 35th St, New York NY 10001; 212 244 3336), 1990; updated edition, Hill & Wang (NY), 1991.

Necessary Illusions: Thought Control in Democratic Societies. South End, 1989.

The Culture of Terrorism. South End, 1988.

Language and Politics. Edited by C.P. Otero. Black Rose Books (distributed by the University of Toronto Press, 340 Nagel Dr, Cheektowaga NY 14225, 716 683 4547), 1988.

Manufacturing Consent (Edward S. Herman, principal author). Pantheon Books (NY), 1988.

Pirates and Emperors: International Terrorism In the Real World. Black Rose, 1986; new edition, Amana (Box 678, Brattleboro VT 05301; 802 257 0872), 1988.

The Chomsky Reader. Edited by James Peck. Pantheon, 1987.

On Power and Ideology: the Managua Lectures. South End, 1987.

Turning the Tide: U.S. Intervention in Central America and the Struggle for Peace. South End, 1985.

The Fateful Triangle: The United States, Israel and the Palestinians. South End, 1983.

Towards a New Cold War. Pantheon, 1982.

Radical Priorities. Black Rose, 1981.

After the Cataclysm: Postwar Indochina and the Reconstruction of Imperial Ideology [The Political Economy of Human Rights, Part II] (with Edward S. Herman). South End, 1979.

Language and Responsibility (interviews with Mitsou Ronat). Pantheon, 1979.

The Washington Connection and Third World Fascism [The Political Economy of Human Rights, Part I] (with Edward S. Herman). South End, 1979.

Peace in the Middle East? Reflections on Justice and Nationhood. Pantheon, 1974 (out of print).

For Reasons of State. Pantheon, 1973 (out of print).

The Pentagon Papers, Volume 5, Analytic Essays and Index (edited with Howard Zinn). Beacon, 1972 (out of print).

Problems of Knowledge and Freedom (the Russell Lectures). Vintage Books (NY), 1972 (out of print).

At War with Asia: Essays on Indochina. Pantheon, 1970 (out of print).

American Power and the New Mandarins. Pantheon, 1969 (out of print).

Index

If you liked this book, check out some of our others:

The CIA's Greatest Hits   Mark Zepezauer

In crisply written, two-page chapters, each accompanied by a cartoon, this book describes the CIA's many attempts to assassinate democracy all over the world. *95 pp. $6.*   *Just out.*

What Uncle Sam Really Wants   Noam Chomsky

A brilliant overview of the real motivations behind US foreign policy, from the man the *New York Times* called "arguably the most important intellectual alive." Chomsky's most popular book, it's full of astounding information. *111 pp. $5.* *Highly recommended. —Booklist*

> **69,000 copies in print**

The Prosperous Few and the Restless Many
Noam Chomsky

A wide-ranging state-of-the-world report that covers everything from Bosnia to NAFTA. Chomsky's fastest-selling book ever, it was on the *Village Voice Literary Supplement*'s bestsellers list for six months running. *95 pp. $5.* *Calmly reasoned. Most welcome. —Newsday*

> **54,000 copies in print**

The Decline and Fall of the American Empire
Gore Vidal

Gore Vidal is one of our most important—and wittiest—social critics. This delightful little book is the perfect introduction to his political views. *95 pp. $5.* *Acerbic, deliciously, maliciously funny.*
      —New York Times Book Review

The Greenpeace Guide to Anti-environmental Organizations   Carl Deal

A comprehensive guide to more than 50 industry front groups that masquerade as environmental organizations. The deception is amazing. *110 pp. $5.* *Fascinating. A must. —New Orleans Times-Picayune*